America
Outside
the World

Other Books
by Louis René Beres

The Management of World Power: A Theoretical Analysis (1973)

Reordering the Planet: Constructing Alternative World Futures, coauthor (1974)

Transforming World Politics: The National Roots of World Peace (1975)

Planning Alternative World Futures: Values, Methods and Models, coauthor (1975)

Terrorism and Global Security: The Nuclear Threat (1979, second edition 1987)

Apocalypse: Nuclear Catastrophe in World Politics (1980)

People, States and World Order (1981)

Mimicking Sisyphus: America's Countervailing Nuclear Strategy (1983)

Reason and Realpolitik: U.S. Foreign Policy and World Order (1984)

Security or Armageddon: Israel's Nuclear Strategy (1986)

America
Outside
the World
The Collapse of U.S. Foreign Policy

by

LOUIS RENÉ BERES

Lexington Books

D.C. Heath and Company • Lexington, Massachusetts • Toronto

Library of Congress Cataloging-in-Publication Data

Beres, Louis René.
America outside the world.

Includes index.
1. United States—Foreign relations—1981–
I. Title.
E876.B466   1987   327.73   86-45598
ISBN-0-669-14016-3 (alk. paper)

Published simultaneously in Canada
Printed in the United States of America
International Standard Book Number: 0-669-14016-3
Library of Congress Catalog Card Number: 86-45598

The paper used in this publication meets
the minimum requirements of American National Standard
for Information Sciences—Permanence of Paper
for Printed Library Materials, ANSI Z39.48-1984.

ISBN 0-669-14016-3

87 88 89 90 8 7 6 5 4 3 2 1

For America

Contents

Acknowledgments

I N preparing this book I have been the beneficiary of help from several sources. Once again I am enormously indebted to my editor, Jaime Welch-Donahue, for gracing my efforts with important insights and heartfelt encouragement. Special thanks at Lexington Books are also due Marsha Finley for her fine work as production editor and Nancy Herndon for valuable assistance as copyeditor. David A. Caputo, my friend and Purdue chairman, maintained the supportive departmental environment without which serious scholarship would have been impossible. At Purdue University I also gratefully acknowledge the outstanding aid of Deanna Johns, who diligently and cheerfully typed the first draft of the manuscript, and Marcy Rhodes, who conscientiously and carefully typed the final version. I am especially fortunate to have the intellectual companionship of my Purdue colleague Michael A. Weinstein, who has taught me a great deal about the individuated life and its implications for world order. From him I have learned much about what Nietzsche called the obligation to "be skilled in living on mountains" and about the primacy of Unamuno's "man of flesh and bone." I alone, of course, bear responsibility for these disturbing yet hopeful thoughts on the relationship between society and statecraft in America.

Introduction

M Y purpose in writing this book is to restore America to the
world. For now, America exists outside the world, in defiance
of its global obligations. It betrays both its traditions and potentialities in a frenzied search for power. As a result, it displays only
impotence.

American foreign policy is deformed and misdirected. At one
level, the reason is obvious. Every component of our international
relations is conceived and presented from the perspective of an all-
consuming anti-Sovietism. I am not suggesting that the Soviet
Union is a decently governed society (indeed it is not) or that we
have no legitimate points of competition with it (indeed we have),
but obsession and caricature in global affairs are invariably self-
defeating.

"The United States has two Soviet problems," writes the political
scientist Stephen F. Cohen. "One is the real but manageable Soviet
threat to our national security and international interests. The second, and increasingly more serious, problem is Sovietophobia, or
exaggerated fear of that Soviet threat."[1] Before America can return
to the world, we must be liberated from this "Sovietophobia." And
before we can expect such liberation, individual Americans will need
to discover the way back to themselves.

Self-liberation is the key to national liberation in America. By
themselves, indictments of Sovietophobia cannot create a purposeful
U.S. foreign policy. Rather, these indictments must be founded on
an authentic understanding of America's ritualized hatred of another
country, an understanding that points toward essential transformations of personal and collective life *within the United States*.

The sounds of "happiness" and "success" in today's America are the dull vibrations of rehearsed gaiety, of false communion, of flight to the herd for meaning and for self-esteem. This reign of the herd instinct flows from a far-reaching assembly of nonpersons, one that takes the images of a surreal world politics for reality, never permitting the world within to assert itself. It should not be surprising, then, that almost an entire nation now accepts gibberish as truth and that a state that seems outwardly powerful and vital is internally decayed, rotten, and about to collapse.

Let us look more closely. What do we see? From Washington and Madison Avenue (they are actually the same place) we witness the endless recitation of fantasy dressed up as fact, the steady naturalistic presentation of an imaginary world rendered believable through repetition. War is peace! A deterrence strategy of "nuclear warfighting" will make us safe from nuclear war. Our European allies must "love the bomb." Civilian populations in America can survive a nuclear war by following government directives for "crisis relocation." Shipping U.S. arms to state sponsors of terrorism will combat anti-American terrorism. Terrorism is counterterrorism!

Borges, the Argentinean writer, tells us that "if we attend the theater, we know that, amid the scenery, there are costumed people speaking the words of Shakespeare or Ibsen or Pirandello, which have been put in their mouths. But we accept that these people are not costumed, that the man in the antechamber slowly talking to himself of vengeance really is Hamlet, Prince of Denmark."[2] We lose ourselves in the theater. Sadly, we also lose ourselves as playgoers attending the absurd drama of politics. Taking actors as authentic leaders, we allow them to play their parts without interference. Acknowledging its willful suspension of disbelief, America forfeits both its interests and its ideals. *Exeunt omnes.*

It is time for a new cast of characters, for *dramatis personae* who will always remain recognizable as performers. First, however, the audience must change, transforming itself from passive observer to active director. This in turn requires a wholly new view of the drama itself, one wherein every important cue has its origins in the individual.

According to Hobbes's *Leviathan* (chap. 16), "A PERSON is he, *whose words or actions are considered, either as his own, or as representing the words or actions of another man. . . .* When they are considered as his owne, then he is called a *Naturall Person:* And when they are considered as representing the words and actions of another, then is he a *Feigned* or *Artificiall person.*" Today's American is only rarely a "Naturall Person." Rather, taking his or her cues from the obligatory discourse of the ritualized public world, the American willingly accepts being "Artificiall" as the price of belonging. Rejecting the essential pact between mind and collectivity, the American surrenders both self and country to defilement and disappearance.

"Collectivities," observed Simone Weil, "do not think; thought only takes shape in a mind that is alone face to face with itself."[3] This is the mind that we must seek. This is the only mind that can restore America to the world.

For now the I, as subject, has vanished. For now the state preempts thought. No one can criticize seriously without first protesting his or her patriotism. This leads to a reminder of just how fortunate the critic is to live within this state, bringing dishonor upon the criticism and shame upon the critic. In the end the state itself falls victim to this syndrome, its dire circumstances an ironic mirror image of the individuals crushed by governmental machinery or by its unwitting servants.

For now we live with the residue of Hegel. The freedom granted to citizens in America is routinely transmuted into obedience. The state is taken as the true self in which the mere individual must be absorbed.

For now nothing is more distasteful for America than to take the path that leads to itself, to its principles, to those purposes for which the authors of the Declaration of Independence pledged "to each other our Lives, our Fortunes and our sacred Honor." Yet it is only by taking this path that we can hope to endure. Exploding the closed universe of a foreign policy that indefatigably patronizes itself, we must recognize ourselves as the vital starting point for a primary victory as a nation, the victory of not perishing.

The I, as subject, must reappear. Captivity by the crowd is a loveless captivity. Nothing can be more monstrous or heartrending. And nothing can be more destructive for America.

How exactly have we gone wrong? What must be done? To answer these questions, this book examines both the origins of our present misfortune and the particular manifestations of suppressed individuality in American foreign policy. From Central America to

South Africa, from global nuclear war to nuclear war in the Middle East, from terrorism to genocide, we will discover the core problem of American foreign policy in the behavior of individuals.

Chapter 1 explains how obsessive anti-Sovietism undermines our interests as a nation. Spawned by the flight from self to the herd, our obsession reflects a devastating bargain between citizens and state. With this bargain, privilege is exchanged for silence and death overtakes life.

Where it is misunderstood, as is the case in America, privilege can be a terrible misfortune. Taken as a payoff for loyalty to the herd and renunciation of self, it crushes individuality and sanctifies the state. In the end such privilege permits governments to proceed with policies that can bring only humiliation and omnicide.

In America privilege has always been misunderstood. H. G. Wells, in *The Future In America*, noted that "the typical American has no 'sense of state.'"[4] By this he did not mean that this American is not passionately and vigorously patriotic (quite the contrary), but that the connections between private searches for affluence and public authority processes are unknown. Said Wells: "I mean that he has no perception that his business activities, his private employments, are constituents in a large collective process; that they affect other people and the world forever, and cannot, as he imagines, begin and end with him."[5]

As the foundation of American foreign policy, realpolitik and its attendant anti-Sovietism are a prescription for necropolis, time-dishonored, long-beaten, routed from survival by a history of crimes and errors. But before we can build on new and more auspicious foundations, Americans will have to cultivate what Wells described as a sense of state, an awareness that certain forms of personal prosperity are always the result of a bargain, and that the costs of this bargain will be both terrible and universal. For now such cultivation lies beyond the pale of the possible, hindered by the ready availability of wealth to some who keep silent. It will become possible, as we shall see, only when economies fail and promises are no longer kept.

Chapters 2 and 3 focus on the errors of U.S. foreign policy in two vital regions: South Africa and Central America. Chapter 4 considers these errors, with particular reference to the multiple threats of nuclear war, in another critical region, the Middle East. This chapter is both region and problem oriented. Chapters 5 and 6 are altogether problem centered, considering the persistent threats of terrorism and genocide that (together with nuclear war) mock our pretensions as a civilized species.

Chapter 7 continues our examination of the problem of nuclear war by directly focusing on war between the superpowers (chapter 4 deals primarily with nuclear conflict between states in the Middle East and only indirectly with "catalytic" nuclear war between the United States and the Soviet Union). Chapter 7 differs from the other chapters in its orientation to the future, which is *retrospective*. Offered in the year 2010, it "looks back" to the present moment, describing in some detail those changes that made possible far-reaching patterns of denuclearization and global harmony. Perhaps, if it is taken seriously, someone in 2010 will write a similar chapter that is not merely an oblique prescription but rather an authentic description of what has already transpired.

Chapter 8 reminds the reader of the personal imperative to transform U.S. foreign policy—an obligation to escape the fatal limitations of theological anti-Sovietism by discovering self-worth outside the herd—and seeks to uncover the essential steps to becoming a person. Significantly, these steps do not lie in the realm of politics, but in the more primary realms of the home, the school, and the work place.

What are these steps? Those who look for precise and exhaustive identification in this book will be disappointed. Such identification is the task of another book, one that must build on the foundations established here. In the end, America's rescue from a self-destroying foreign policy will require a fusion of international relations with sociology and child development as a whole new field of study.

Such a fusion will have to pay close attention to the education of persons. Discarding current emphases on vocationalism and career training, it will aim at the development of human beings rather than citizens. As Rousseau observed in *Emile*, a masterpiece of educational reform that has yet to be taken seriously: "The natural man lives for himself; he is the unit, the whole, dependent only on himself and on his like. The citizen is but the numerator of a fraction, whose value depends on its denominator; his value depends upon the whole, that is, on the community. Good social institutions are those best fitted to make a man unnatural, to exchange his independence for dependence, to merge the unit in the group."[6]

Of course, Rousseau does not urge the abandonment of community. Rather, he understands that true community can never be built on "numerators," on people who are afraid to become themselves. In choosing a path to education, "you must make your choice between the man and the citizen, you cannot train both."

Life is the trade Rousseau wishes us all to be taught. When the student leaves his teachers, "he will be neither a magistrate, a soldier, nor a priest; he will be a man." This is the kind of education that must be explored further if America is to be returned to itself.

We must also look at work. "All his life long," says Rousseau, "man is imprisoned by our institutions," and today there is no place more confining than the work place. In America, even the more fortunate workers are typically reduced to machine tenders or paper shufflers, and high-status professionals are forever reminded that their value lies in being members of the "team." Not surprisingly, individuals only rarely envision the larger purpose of their work efforts, a condition that splinters all residual sense of self and mandates withdrawal to the herd.

The results are ominous. Ground down by both their education and their jobs, Americans have grown accustomed to "belonging." As feelings of self-worth are established according to the standards of these primary institutions (which are also reaffirmed by the family), these standards are not treated lightly. When the state demands similar and even greater expressions of loyalty, it is not disappointed. Prepared in the nonpolitical spheres of home, school, and job for the obligations of "citizenship," we quickly learn that without cooperation there is only estrangement and failure.

Americans are "free," if by freedom we mean only a relation to the political sphere. But what is the value of political freedom if our social institutions imprison our selves? This question was already raised by the American transcendentalist Henry David Thoreau more than one hundred years ago:

> America is said to be the arena on which the battle of freedom is to be fought; but surely it cannot be freedom in a merely political sense that is meant. Even if we grant that the American has freed himself from a political tyrant, he is still the slave of an economical

and moral tyrant. Now that the republic—the *res-publica*—has been settled, it is time to look after the *res-private*—the private state—to see, as the Roman senate charged its consuls, "*ne quid res-PRIVATA detrimenti caperet*," that the *private* state receive no detriment.[7]

"Do we call this the land of the free?" asked Thoreau. "We quarter our gross bodies on our poor souls, till the former eat up all the latter's substance."[8] Thoreau had ample reason for pessimism (as we have today), but it is still too early to despair. Indeed, this book rests on the presumption that America, for all of its blemishes, remains the last hope for an entire planet. With the artist John Butler Yeats, father of the poet, I can agree that "hope the great divinity is domiciled in America."[9]

Notes

1. See Stephen F. Cohen, *Sovieticus: American Perceptions and Soviet Realities* (New York: W. W. Norton, 1986), 17.
2. See Jorge Luis Borges, *Seven Nights*, trans. Eliot Weinberger (New York: New Directions, 1984), 12–13.
3. See Simone Weil, *Oppression and Liberty*, trans. Arthur Wills and John Petrie (Amherst: University of Massachusetts Press, 1973), 98.
4. See Marc Pachter, ed., *Abroad in America: Visitors to the New Nation 1776–1914* (Reading, Mass.: Addison-Wesley in association with the National Portrait Gallery, Smithsonian Institution, 1976), 298.
5. Ibid.
6. The citations from Rousseau are taken from *Emile*, book 1, trans. Barbara Foxley, (London: Dent, 1963). *Emile* was written between 1757 and 1760 and was first published in 1762.
7. Thoreau, "Life Without Principle," *Atlantic Monthly* (October 1863); cited from Perry Miller, ed., *The American Transcendentalists* (Garden City, N.Y.: Doubleday, 1957), 324–25.
8. Ibid., 325.
9. Cited in Pachter, *Abroad in America*, ix.

1

Status and Statecraft in the United States: The Origins of Our Misfortune

> And now what shall become of us without any barbarians?
> Those people were a kind of solution.
>
> — Cavafy, "Expecting the Barbarians"

I N the longest of our imaginable perspectives, the United States will certainly disappear. This is a trivial observation, one hardly worth mentioning. What is uncertain is the amount of time that must pass before we are erased.

Can anything be done to extend our time? Or is it already too late? As a nation languishing at the abyss, can we foresee any other end but apocalypse? Fatalists have a simple answer: *Après nous, le déluge*. Our leaders approach annihilation as healer. Let us not think. It will only disturb our sleep.

Others, however, have yet to surrender. Refusing to be sacrificed to our dominant orthodoxy, they seek refuge in a new world politics, a rhythm of compassion and consciousness that can prolong our days. More than anything else, it is a rhythm of fraternity between the superpowers.

But this is naive. It is preposterous. The United States and the Soviet Union have always been enemies. They must continue to be enemies. No less an authority than former U.S. National Security Adviser Robert C. McFarlane tells us, "We don't plan policy in the expectation of transforming East-West relations."[1]

For if the Soviet Union did not exist our leaders would have to invent it. Otherwise, to whom would we feel superior? To whom would we impute our frustrations, our weaknesses, our failures? To what ends would we feel compelled to sustain the prevailing institutions of power?

Anti-Sovietism serves only short-term special interests. On examination it reveals its own insubstantiality. Allegedly the only pragmatic approach to world affairs, it is in fact unremittingly utopian.

We conjure up enemies because we are not at peace with ourselves. Yet ridden by the fear of ineffectuality, we find little solace in hatred of another society. Deprived of values that are "graspable," that touch the heart and make us feel alive, we seek comfort where comfort can never be: in a world that increasingly resembles a huge bomb shelter, walled with nuclear weapons.

The American supporter of anti-Sovietism is fearful of discovering that the world is ill-contrived, with many causes for its multiple misfortunes, for then he or she would be obliged to understand and master a complicated reality. Rather than be burdened with an agonizing responsibility, this American localizes all evil in a concrete adversary. Left unimpeded such views will have a self-fulfilling effect, creating the conditions under which one superpower or the other, or both, must be removed.

At its heart the problem is one of individuals. Our leaders can exploit an anti-Soviet world view only because this satisfies the particular cravings of people. By treating the Soviet Union as a pernicious society, Americans affirm that *they* belong to an elite, one that is based on goodness. There are no special requirements for membership in this elite, no standards of excellence that must be met, only citizenship in the United States.

Everything in American society reveals loneliness. Despite feverish commitments to being "in," virtually everyone feels "out." Fearful of responding to personal cues of purposeful behavior, Americans react only to the shallow and degrading calls of the crowd. Instead of moving toward a society of real power and dignity, we surrender to somnambulism, immobilized by a despotism every bit as pernicious as political dictatorship.

The human roots of American statecraft are inextricably intertwined with the dynamics of status and self-worth in personal relations. The individual American supports a protracted enmity with the Soviet Union largely out of fear of being alone. To this end, he or she finds the existence of the Evil Empire absolutely necessary. Small matter that the Soviet Union is essentially a state like his or her own, comprised of people like himself or herself. Driven to devalue reason at the outset, the American is impervious to logic, responding only to the strong emotional benefits of belonging.

The American who accepts such a view may readily confess that the Soviet counterpart shares a basic humanity. But this concession costs nothing, for the American has put this quality in parentheses. What matters is that a condition of sustained international enmity overcomes solitariness and mediocrity, that it enobles membership in the herd. This membership, however, destroys the very element of individuality that we require. Consider the chief character in Andre Gide's *The Immoralist*, who notes: "People are afraid to find themselves alone, and don't find themselves at all . . . what seems different in yourself: that's the one rare thing you possess, the one thing that gives each of us his worth; and that's just what we try to suppress. We imitate."

It follows from this that before the United States can extricate itself from the predatory embrace of anti-Sovietism, individual Americans will need to discover alternative and more authentic sources of reassurance. To a certain extent this process is already underway, animated by the manifestly contrived dualism offered by our leaders. Yet the benefits of this process will accrue only to those people who display some measure of political awareness and will be lost on the many millions of others who are unmoved by reason.

What is to be done about those for whom the angst of our time is only the newest form of hubris? Although their politics is a lie, confirming a total disjunction between problem and solution, it is a politics that confers essential ego satisfaction and self-esteem. What are appropriate substitute forms of satisfaction?

To answer these questions we must understand that the journey from ubiquitous conformity to personhood begins with myth and ends with apprehension. To complete this journey the individual must learn to substitute a system of uncertainties for what he or she has always believed, to encourage doubt as a replacement for the comforting woes of clichés and slogans. Induced to live against the grain of our shallow civilization, the individual must become not only conscious of his or her singularity but satisfied with it. Organ-ically separated from the herd, he or she must embrace the forces that undermine it, forces that offer a last remaining chance for both meaning and survival.

What are these forces? They are warnings that disturb confidence in the present moment, that remind us of our imprisonment. Although it is true that we enjoy, as Americans, a high degree of conventional political freedoms, it is also true that we are in a larger sense captives. Bought off by the promises of participation and production, we have exchanged our capacity to act as individuals for the security of centrally directed automata. Enveloped by the comforting fog of "representative government," we have become unwilling to question.

The danger was foreseen by Tocqueville, who understood that democracy can produce its own forms of tyranny. Tocqueville envisioned a benignly operating polity that "hinders, restrains, enervates, stifles and stultifies" by imposing "a network of petty complicated rules." Encouraging the citizen to pursue "petty and banal pleasures," and "to exist in and for himself," democratic "equality" has set the stage for isolation and passivity.[2]

Thus much of our freedom is an illusion. Indeed, we contribute to our unfreedom as individuals because we don't recognize the extent of our captivity. As Rousseau writes in *Emile*: "There is no subjugation so perfect as that which keeps the appearance of freedom, for in that way one captures volition itself."

This brings us to the core of the problem. Bereft of volition, we are almost reflexively obedient, ever ready to defer. Captivated by the delusion of potency and autonomy, we have surrendered to impotence and passionless automatism. Overwhelmed by a burlesque chorus of national cheerleaders, we seek shelter in thoughtlessness.

Thoughtlessness is rewarded: it is a virtue of the "good citizen." Benedetto Croce spoke of the strange duty of citizens *not to think*. Invoked in the name of faith, such "duty" retards personhood and destroys the nation. Today, even many of the best-educated Americans live in intellectual stupor, tolerating the most colossal inner contradictions for the sake of belonging.

But why such a desperate need to belong? The answer lies in our incapacity to find self-worth within ourselves. This incapacity, in turn, is nurtured by a society that positively despises self-liberation. Offering a cornucopia of "things" to those who maintain proper faith, this society is determined to cancel the individual.

The shape of this society has been taking form for many years. Sailing to New York from Dublin in 1907, John Butler Yeats explained to the critic and scholar Oliver Elton the problem of America: "What America needs to rescue it from its unrest and its delerious collectivism is poets and solitaries, men who turn aside and live to themselves and enjoy the luxury of their own feelings and thoughts. Poets here are orators—have to be so, since the public is their paymaster and ready to pay them handsomely if only they will desert their caves of solitary personal feeling and come out and work for their generous and affectionate masters."[3]

The caves, of course, are generally empty. We see in America today an unbridled concern for affluence coexisting with growing expressions of pain. The president of the United States has declared war on drugs, but this war ignores the fundamental questions of *cause*. Why do so many Americans, who have so much, feel such pain? Why has the "successful" quest for the "good life" produced so much in the way of unhappiness?

The answer to these questions lies in the continuing dispossession of the individual by the collectivity. Although we are free to a remarkable degree from ordinary patterns of political repression, we have yet to be liberated as individuals. We are as free as sheep. "Of what use is it to sheep that no one abridges their freedom of speech?" asked Max Stirner. "They stick to bleating."[4]

In many respects our oppression as Americans is greater than the oppression of many other peoples throughout history, including several of those we describe as enslaved. Never before has a single society been more vulnerable to instant disappearance. And never before have individual members of a society been less effectual in producing a change that could bring survival.

Controlled by a popular press and media that make thinking almost impossible, individual Americans remain quiet in the world, living in it tentatively, as if it were not theirs. George Orwell's gloomy prophecy in *1984* described a world of sophisticated surveillance techniques and the disappearance of privacy, a world where Big Brother watched all but was himself invisible. Ironically, the homogenizing and socializing effect of TV and the electronic media now make such control unnecessary. Americans don't need to be kept in line by external political constraints. As they have been baptized into a singular political theology from earliest childhood, the possibilities for serious dissent, for heresy, never surface.[5]

By its forfeiture of individuality a whole nation now swallows its breakfast cereals with a hodgepodge of ready-made opinions, a common store of images that conceals thoughtlessness in a frenzy of mimicry. The fact that these opinions are often absurd, humiliating, and deformed—and are always the product of an impoverished imagination—is rarely even considered. The delusions are comforting. They perpetuate themselves endlessly and effortlessly.

"The mass media," says Michael A. Weinstein, "make the imagination thoroughly reproductive, rummaging in the storehouse of memory for any images that might evoke a sentimental response and finally feeding off their own reproductions."[6] In such a society, which blocks access to more genuine images of meaning and self-worth, it is hardly surprising to find so much unhappiness, so many citizens anesthetizing themselves to the pain of inauthenticity with drugs and empty voyeurism. In such a society, the lethal vulgarity of the herd manifests itself in everything from sexual profligacy to random violence, and reverberates in every action that we take or resist.

To change all this—and to place America *inside* the world—we must first return to ourselves. Hope remains, but it must sing in an undertone. We must study history, but not in an atmosphere of false greatness. To grasp the lessons of history, we must first despise false greatness. As we learn from Simone Weil: "How should a child who sees cruelty and ambition glorified in his history lessons; egoism, pride, vanity, passion for self-advertisement glorified in his literature lessons; all the discoveries that have unsettled the lives of men glorified in his science lessons, without any account being taken of either the method of discovery or the effect of the unsettlement produced—how should he be expected to admire the good?"[7]

A bargain has been struck! Americans are free as a *people*, but only at the price of self-renunciation. The individual American who seeks true greatness within himself, apart from his membership in the state, is subject to ostracism and exclusion. Athens, as Max Stirner noted, precisely at its freest moment created ostracism, banished the atheists, and poisoned the most honest thinker.[8]

The ironies abound. Our capitulation to an all-consuming anti-

Sovietism is made possible by the guarantees of a democratic society. However, these guarantees need not be the source of our debility as a people and as a nation. Taken as a starting point for a challenge to current foreign policies—a point for which they were originally intended—they could contribute to our personal and collective liberation.

But a renewed awareness of political freedom is not enough. We must first understand that the rewards of compliance are unsatisfactory, that they are erected on the deception that self-worth flows freely from personal wealth and unceasing consumption.[9] Such an understanding is already underway, animated by wave after wave of dissatisfaction with the trappings of "success."

This dissatisfaction has been well documented; sociologists have constructed entire libraries of Ph.D. theses on the topic. One engaging comment was offered by the novelist Walker Percy. In a literary career that spans the publication of his novel *The Moviegoer* in 1961 through the publication of his second work of nonfiction, *Lost in the Cosmos: The Last Self-Help Book*, in 1983, Percy's chief concern has been with "the dislocation of man in the modern age." Struck by the sense of ennui and meaninglessness that shadows lives nestled in affluence, Percy tells one interviewer: "The thing that fascinates me is the fact that men can be well-off, judging by their own criteria, with all their needs satisfied, goals achieved, et cetera, yet as time goes on, life is almost unbearable. Amazing!"[10]

But it is not really amazing. In late twentieth century America metaphysic is replaced by myth. Deprived of anything remotely resembling an authentic creed, Americans seek solace in silence. Yet in trading off their freedom to disobey for an expanding array of consumer goods, they inevitably discover unhappiness. It is not that they recognize the *idee fixe* of anti-Sovietism as a lie (they have never really been interested in foreign affairs as such), but that their reward for "going along" is not what it was cut out to be.

The problem has been captured with particular insight by Amos Oz, the Israeli writer:

America has promoted and spread all over the world the simple ideal of individual happiness. Various religions, civilizations and ideologies throughout history regarded happiness as a collective rather than an individual experience. Almost all of them are losing ground to that triumphant American vision of private happiness. Hundreds of millions of people, from Tokyo to Leningrad, from Cairo to Buenos Aires, dream of being happy in the American way. Sometimes they dream of being happily American. But is the new global America, this international happiness-oriented village, a happy place? I'm afraid I can only propose an un-American answer to this highly American question. The popular American dream of living happily ever after, while dazzling the world, reminds me of the American landscape itself: plentiful, elusive, and forlorn.[11]

Despite the balloons and bravado of "a new patriotism," the spectacle of America today is one of nihilism. Not daring to look our approaching disappearance in the face, we have surrendered to an unprecedented form of gluttony, an insatiable craving for more and more that produces nothing in the way of satisfaction. Desperate to demonstrate our principles and our power, we succeed only in buttressing injustice and in abdicating our influence. Bereft of an authentic vital energy, we have turned from the possibilities of wisdom and genuine understanding to a desolate panorama of superstition, trivia, endless consumption, and cheap taste.

We live longer, but for what reasonable purpose? The extra years are for the most part without personal or collective benefit. Even our hedonism is contrived. According to Octavio Paz: "Our hedonism is a hedonism for robots and wraiths. Viewing the body as merely a mechanism leads to the mechanization of pleasure; in its turn, the cult of the image—movies, television, advertising—gives rise to a sort of generalized voyeurism that converts bodies into shadows. Our materialism is not carnal; it is an abstraction."[12]

For most Americans, the failure of the present lies not in the vacant intuitions of our leaders (for this has always been manifest to anyone who cares to notice) but in the disappointing exchange of "things" for silence. In an era where there is no meaningful difference between the boardrooms of our major corporations and the backrooms of organized crime, it is not that we expect honesty, but that we feel cheated by the bargain we have struck. We are sickened when we hear our leaders brandish cosmic principles of "freedom" and "democracy" with evangelical fervor, not because we have ever taken such mendacities of language seriously, but because we have felt no compensation for our dishonor.

The barbarians are not outside the gates. They are ourselves. We stand ready to bring about total collapse unless we learn to rebel. This rebellion must not be directed against our political order (the ordinary meaning of rebellion), but against the underlying oppression of a stultifying society.

What kind of a society is it?

1. It is a society in which a survey (1986) of nearly 2,000 high-achieving students revealed that 46 percent knew a young person who had committed suicide or tried to commit suicide, and 31 percent said they've contemplated it themselves.

2. It is a society in which the principal problem in the schools is a "crack" epidemic.

3. It is a society in which some 30 million Americans smoke marijuana regularly, amounting to 130,000 pounds used daily in the United States (enough to keep most of the population mildly stoned).

4. It is a society of "designer drugs."

5. It is a society with a steadily growing population of cocaine-addicted babies.

6. It is a society where some of Hitler's surviving weapons designers are now leading U.S. advocates of Star Wars.

7. It is a society where drive-in funeral homes cater to the bereaved-but-busy (one drives up, signs a condolence card, pulls ahead to the viewing window for a moment of silence, and exits into traffic—elapsed time: 30 seconds).

8. It is a society where a chief justice of the United States owns deeds to properties with covenants barring nonwhites and Jews.

9. It is a society exploding with films that caricature the Soviet Union and dehumanize its population.

10. It is a society in which television is the primal force, sealed-off, self-contained, hurling coded messages that suggest "critical issues" for our time . . . Coke is it, Coke is it, Coke is it.

11. It is a society in which teens during grades 7–12 listen to an average of 10,500 hours of rock music, the lyrics of which have never been more sexually explicit and violent.

12. It is a society in which sales of war toys have increased 600 percent since 1982, making the war toys industry worth well over a billion dollars (more than 218 million war toys and accessories were sold in 1985, roughly five for every child in the United States.

13. It is a society in which dolls with names like Ripsaw, Flashfists, Twinblade, Slice, and Clawgut come equipped with multiple machine guns, particle-beam cannons, and nuclear-powered laser guns.

14. It is a society in which according to the National Coalition on Television Violence, the average American child is now exposed to 250 cartoons with war themes and 800 television advertisements for war toys a year.

15. It is a society in which by the age of sixteen the average child has watched some 20,000 hours of TV, taking in 200,000 acts of violence and 50,000 attempted murders—33,000 of which involve guns.

16. It is a society with an estimated 500,000 unregistered military-style assault guns.

17. It is a society where abandoned toxic waste dumps pose a danger to the health and well-being of millions, air pollution has reached staggering proportions, acid rain has damaged millions of acres of forest land and has killed thousands of lakes and streams, and even tap water is largely unsafe to drink.

18. It is a society in which influence peddling is a major growth industry, the center of lobbying activity on Capitol Hill is known as Gucci Gulch after the expensive Italian shoes, and former administration officials are often paid millions of dollars by special interests to oppose policies they once ardently promoted.

19. It is a society where one in four American preschool children grows up in poverty, more than half of all births to teen mothers are out of wedlock, and by 1997 the majority of seventeen-year-olds will come from broken homes.

20. It is a society where U.S. defense contracts are awarded to foreign companies connected to states that support anti-American terrorism.

21. It is a society that accepts huge reductions in federal spending (FY 1988) for clean air, clean water, and the removal of asbestos from public elementary schools.

22. It is a society that urges its young men to "fight for your country" while it simultaneously reduces (FY 1988) veterans' benefits.

23. It is a society that spends 170 times as much public research money for transport into space as for mass transit on earth.

24. It is a society in which one person out of six may bear the scars of serious childhood sexual abuse.

25. It is a society that has built up a public debt exceeding $2,000 billion, doubling during the Reagan presidency.

26. It is a society that ranks (among 142 countries) first in arms exports, military expenditures, nuclear warheads, and bombs, but fourth in literacy rate, seventh in life expectancy, tenth in public education expenditures per capita, tenth in public health expenditures per capita, fourteenth in percent population with safe water, seventeenth in infant mortality rate, seventeenth in percent of women in university enrollment, and twenty-second in population per physician.[13]

27. It is a society in which the U.S. Conference of Mayors reported in 1985 that one-fifth of the requests for emergency food could not be met, and that in half of the big cities shelters routinely turn away homeless people for lack of space.

28. It is a society in which an increasing shortage of low-cost housing has raised the estimated number of homeless people to between 350,000 and 3 million.

29. It is a society in which, between 1980 and 1985, the largest increase in people seeking shelter in urban centers was among families with children.

30. It is a society in which the number of people living below the poverty threshold increased from 29 million in 1980 to 33 million in 1985, about 14 percent of the population.

31. It is a society in which about 35 million Americans have neither private nor government-sponsored health insurance.

32. It is a society in which, in a single year, one million families were refused medical care for financial reasons.

33. It is a society in which infant mortality rates in the inner cities rank with high rates in some of the poorest countries of the Caribbean.

34. It is a society in which an estimated 20 million Americans are without adequate nutrition on a regular basis, despite the fact that the United States is the largest food-producing nation in the world.

35. It is a society in which the share of total income going to the poorest 20 percent of the population has dropped to 4.7 percent, the lowest in twenty-five years, while the share of the richest 20 percent has increased to 42.9 percent, a postwar high.

36. It is a society in which President Reagan can make the following statements without widespread or serious challenge:
    On the environment: "There is today in the United States as much forest as there was when Washington was at Valley Forge."
    On the Contras: "They are the moral equal of our Founding Fathers and the brave men and women of the French Resistance."
    On the military: "You have to remember, we don't have the military-industrial complex we once had."
    On cuts in social services: "My program hasn't hurt anybody."
    On Bitburg and the Nazis: "They were victims, just as surely as the victims in the concentration camps."

"We live," as Camus tells us in the *The Rebel*, "in an unsacrosanct moment in history." If our society continues on its present course, the word *thought* will remain a vulgarity, climaxed, perhaps, by a permanent exile from our national vocabulary. But if an aroused citizenry begins to seek self-worth outside the confines of sanitized shopping malls and prefabricated mass taste, we may still have a chance. Drawing on a new and authentic sense of personal status, we might still transform an ideology of human freedom from hallucination to habit.

How shall we begin this search? Unsuited to the obligations of despair, Americans may draw false warnings from their condition, moving not toward consciousness but surrender. Misunderstanding T. S. Eliot's advice that "it is no longer possible to find consolation in prophetic gloom," we may remain in stupor, preferring even our anesthetized universe to the dark perils of uncertainty.

There is no quick fix to the problem of personhood in our age of compliance, no magic capsule that can cure the pathology in our national and international body politic. The media, on its own, is not about to end its projections of an idealized American life. The schools, always the primary instrument of socialization in the popular culture of obedience, are hardly in the throes of an intellectual awakening. Even the universities, theoretically the most independent sector of society, are nothing more than willing servitors of political and corporate power, ever ready to do what is "realistic." Cadres of apparatchiks, who still dare to call themselves professors, continue the process begun in the elementary school of assiduously suppressing manifestations of self-affirmation wherever they appear.

In 1978 the historian Theodore Roszak wrote, "We live in a time when the very private experience of having a personal identity to discover, a personal destiny to fulfill, has become a subversive political force of major proportions." This observation is even truer today. Lacking the public gestures of impetuosity and self-determination that were still acceptable several years ago, we are forced to become persons in a society that positively despises our individuality, a society whose policy is still "to grind personhood down into rubble and then to remold the pieces into obedient, efficient, and, of course, cheerful personnel."[14]

What shall we do? Roszak wrote that "there is an irresistible fascination to the project of creating an original identity,"[15] but fascination is not enough. We need significant incentives, ones with broad and substantial appeal. Where can they be found?

There is only one answer. The sources of our personal and political transformation lie entirely within those particular individuals who are already aware of our misfortune. Scattered widely across every occupation and profession and in every corner of our country, these repositories of consciousness must exchange purposeful interaction for solitary alienation. Brought together by the imperative to survive, they must become the starting point for a whole new kind of public activity. Rejecting the futile dynamics of partisan domestic politics as a delusion—one that can only consecrate our flirtations with the apocalypse—they must aim at nothing less than real social action and leadership.

This will take time. And in a society that seems to have lost its capacity to imagine alternatives, it will require a fortitude that borders on the sublime. Needed changes carry no guarantees; indeed, they are altogether improbable.

Plato understood the difficulty in getting already conscious sectors of the public to act as a vanguard of change. As he says in the *Republic*: "A man whose thoughts are fixed on true reality has no leisure to look downwards on the affairs of men, to take part in their quarrels, and to catch the infection of their jealousies and hates. He contemplates a world of unchanging and harmonious order, where reason governs and nothing can do or suffer wrong."

Yet faith in new forms of personhood and politics is an essential step toward their implementation. Today idealists and realists have changed places. Confronted with a statecraft that is fashioned on the sordid promise of endless conflict, we must affirm that the truest forms of realism lie in the imaginings of distant possibilities. Time, as St. Augustine wrote, is more than the present as we experience it and the past as a present memory. It is also the future as a present expectation, and this expectation carries within itself the seeds of its own verification.

If all of this discussion of *real* social action sounds grandly naive, it is because politics as usual can never succeed. If it all sounds hopelessly idealistic, we must recognize that nothing can be more fanciful than continuing on the present course. To be sure, those forces that would continue to enslave us through the theology of anti-Sovietism have the edge, but our concession to such an advantage can produce only death.

Jorge Luis Borges writes of a time in the future when politics will disappear and politicians will go on to become either comedians or faith healers (because that is what they are most suited to do). Such time is not yet at hand, and politicians still have to be taken seriously. This is true in both the United States and the Soviet Union.

In the United States, anti-Sovietism is a strategy for public manipulation. Less an ideology than the absence of an ideal, it is exploited by cynical political elites to displace private anguish and to sustain existing patterns of power. A surreal spectrum of clichés masquerading as serious thought, it shamelessly distorts patriotic fervor. The problem has been recognized with particular insight by George Konrad, one of Eastern Europe's most distinguished writers:

In point of fact, it is not ideologies that contend today, nor is it systems like capitalism and communism. Anyone who believes that two systems and two ideologies are pitted against each other today has fallen victim to the secularized metaphysics of our civilization, which looks for a duel between God and Satan in what is, after all, only a game. Russians and Americans—their political classes, that is—circle each other in the ring. Each of the two world heavyweight champions would like to show he is the strongest in the world; they are playing a game with each other whose paraphernalia include nuclear missiles. Yet it is impossible to construct from the Soviet-American conflict an ideological dichotomy along whose axis the values of our continent can be ranged. The antitheses which fill our mental horizon—capitalism versus state socialism, democracy versus totalitarianism, market economy versus planned economy—are forced mythologies which the intelligentsias of East and West either confuse with reality or else, being aware that they are not very precise appellations, seek to square with the real facts.[16]

Our contrived hatred of the Soviet Union points unambiguously toward war. Left unchecked, it will leave only crushed bones as mementos.

Hatred is a powerful emotion. It can even override the strongest forces of human love. It can make a mockery of human reason.

In the play by Euripides, Medea kills her two children to satisfy her hatred for Jason, her husband, because "passion, that cause of direst woes to mortal man, hath triumphed over my sober thoughts." Medea slays the offspring of her womb not because of a craven deficiency in maternal love, but because her hatred of Jason knows no bounds. Indeed, looking upon her children's corpses, she refuses even to accept responsibility, blaming the act upon Jason's "foul treatment" and "feeble lust."

There is a lesson here for the architects of U.S. foreign policy. Although they have constructed an elaborate canon of nuclear deterrence designed to ensure our survival, they have coupled these rules of self-preservation with an obsessive anti-Sovietism. Should these feelings of hatred be inflamed further, the presumed requirements of geopolitical competition might well displace the interests of peace. Hating the Russians even more than they care for us, our leaders are apt at one time or another to bring about nuclear war. When this happens, those who survive (if any do) will disclaim responsibility, blaming the demonic ambitions of an Evil Empire.

When *Medea* was first produced in 431 B. C., the Greek world was about to enter the twenty-seven years of carnage known to us as the Peloponnesian War. Widely accused of impiety, Euripides saw his beloved Athens move relentlessly toward its own destruction, abandoning virtue for the predatory illusions of power. Today we witness a similar decline by the United States as this country's highest ideals and interests are sacrificed to the desolate intuitions of realpolitik.

To survive, the United States must consistently value love over hatred, national self-preservation over the destruction of a despised adversary. Such a commitment to reason is now in jeopardy as anti-Sovietism takes on the character of a new theology. Left unchecked, the bile of hatred for another state can only undermine the delicate balance of terror, provoking a cycle of recklessness and belligerence leading directly toward necropolis. Reflecting glib archeologists of ruins-in-the-making, the subordination of national self-interest to a now sacred form of competition will bring us to the outer limits of misfortune.

A theological element makes current U.S. nuclear strategy especially resistant to challenge. This strategy is rationalized not only by "science" but by quasi-religious fantasies of struggle between the Sons of Light and the Sons of Darkness. Thus, moves to encourage new and far-reaching sources of self-worth that are unsullied by statecraft will be hard to sustain. Change will require not only an illumination of our fragile bases of self-worth in a world dominated by superpower competition, but also a full exposure of the misuses of science and the perversions of faith. As inhabitants of a multistate world, Americans must understand that nuclearism is not reason and that our enemy is not Satan. With such an understanding, we might still reverse the obscene transfer of both science and the sacred to our technology of annihilation, a reversal that would signal the triumph of personhood over the herd, and, ultimately, of life over death.

No one can be safe in America until the market for individual meaning is removed from the sweating palms of the state, until it belongs to the proprietors of awareness. Rejecting the shamans who would deny us our worth apart from the contrived dynamics of endless international belligerence, we must let others know that we were persons only *before* our disfigurement by politics and that we surrendered our personhood the moment we tolerated the lies of official thought. Once this becomes known, the suffocating and destructive propositions of the new theology will collapse into an incoherent heap.

Before this can happen, however, the prophets of a new culture of personal meaning must be willing to speak the truth. Because the power of awareness and the power of the state are irreconcilable, a price must be paid for honoring awareness. In a world where rewards are bestowed upon those who allow themselves to be used as instruments, this price is possible exile from "the good life."

Those who are unwilling to pay this price are, by definition, unsuited for the task. Terrified to offer abilities on their own terms, they remain marionettes of the buyer, content to do stupid work, or—even worse—to degrade the dignity of all others. More dangerous by far, because they understand the deception, than those who have been fooled by the new theology, they are the virtuous lackeys of public authority, the whores of power for whom integrity will always be unbearable.

This problem was perhaps best understood by Hermann Hesse. In the characterless Philistine who epitomizes mediocrity, cowardice, compromise, and servility, Hesse described a creature of strong appetites but no taste, of surface confidence but no ideals, of great zeal and even diligence but no meaningful aspirations. Today the world belongs to this mass-man. Our only hope lies in those who brood and dream at the edges of this world, in those *Phantasie-menschen* (creative dreamers) of Hesse who would reveal the desolation and fragility of a society directed by "solid citizens."

Other problems block the liberation of American society. The promise of an informed public depends on the stature of the intellect. Yet even as the cerebrum is liberating itself, the intellect falls into disrepute. In the United States in particular, receptivity to bold, threatening ideas has never been high.

But the problems are not insurmountable. If they were, the entire enterprise of seeking a transformation of personal and political life would be a cruel hoax, undermining the remnants of happiness without any purpose. Acknowledging the connections between our current foreign policy and the manipulation of false needs, we can begin to understand the causes of our vulnerability—causes that lie in suppressed individuality and that foreshadow oblivion. Rejecting the hollow rewards of complicity, we can move beyond the transparent pantomime of U.S.–Soviet rivalry to a new world politics of dignity and hope.

Speaking of humankind as a whole, Rimbaud once complained that "we are not in the world." So it is with America today. We stand, as a nation, outside the world, drawn to our final rendezvous with extinction because we have steadfastly refused to become persons. How much treasure, how much science, how much labor and planning, how many centuries have we ransacked to make possible the grotesque carnival of nuclear war? Frightened by the stubborn fact of death, how much longer can we extend our denials of mortality from individual to collective levels?

The answers cause pain. Our worship of the state, which allows our leaders to maintain a disastrous course, flows from an unwillingness to seek meaning within ourselves. But by transmuting freedom into obedience, we have created a false god before whom millions (or even billions) will be made to pass through fire. In the end, if we are to endure, our sense of self-worth will have to come from the inside. Recognizing that we must die,[17] and that our mortality cannot be undone through the acquisition of wealth and influence over others, we can begin to celebrate a new life-afffirming ethos of personal value and private meaning—an ethos determined by courage and imagination rather than Washington and Madison Avenue. Only then can we return to a safer course as a nation. Only then can America stand again inside the world.

Notes

1. See Robert C. McFarlane, "U.S.-Soviet Relations in the Late 20th Century," Current Policy No. 733, U.S. Department of State, Bureau of Public Affairs, Washington, D.C., 1985.
2. See Alexis de Tocqueville, *Democracy in America*, trans. George Lawrence (Garden City, N.Y. Doubleday, 1969. Originally published 1835, 692.
3. See Marc Pachter, ed., *Abroad in America: Visitors to the New Nation, 1776–1914* (Reading, Mass.: Addison-Wesley in association with the National Portrait Gallery, Smithsonian Institution, 1976), 268.

4. See Max Stirner, *The Ego and His Own: The Case of the Individual against Authority*, trans. Steven T. Byington (1845; New York: Libertarian Book Club, 1963). A formidable assault on authoritarianism in the mid nineteenth century, Stirner's book represented a "third force"—neither a defender of the theological or monarchical state nor a supporter of models offered by Liberals and Socialists. Conceived as *the* rejoinder to Hegel, it argued that all freedom is essentially self-liberation—an argument that influenced the writing of Henrik Ibsen.

5. For an interesting work on the homogenizing effects of TV and the manner in which they retard personhood, see Joshua Meyrowitz, *No Sense of Place: The Impact of Electronic Media on Social Behavior* (New York: Oxford University Press, 1985). The situational analysis offered by Meyrowitz describes how the electronic media affect social behavior not through the intrinsic power of their messages but by "reorganizing the social settings in which people interact and by weakening the once strong relationship between physical place and social place." (p. ix)

6. See Michael A. Weinstein, "Unamuno on the Normed Imagination," unpublished mimeo, Purdue University (1986), 17.

7. See Simone Weil, *The Need for Roots: Prelude to a Declaration of Duties toward Mankind* (New York: G. P. Putnam's Sons, 1952), 234.

8. See Stirner, *The Ego and His Own*, 214.

9. One is reminded here of the observation by Adam Smith: "The rich man glories in his riches, because he feels that they naturally draw upon him the attention of the world. . . . At the thought of this, his heart seems to swell and dilate itself within him, and he is fonder of his wealth, upon this account, than for all the other advantages it procures him." See Smith, *Theory of Moral Sentiments* (Oxford: Clarendon Press, 1976), 50–51.

10. See Roger Kimball's review of Lewis A. Lawson and Victor A. Kramer, eds., *Conversations With Walker Percy* (Jackson: University Press of Mississippi, 1985), in *New York Times Book Review*, August 4, 1985, 9.

11. From an interview in *Time*, June 16, 1986, 53.

12. See Octavio Paz, *One Earth: Four or Five Worlds: Reflections on Contemporary History*, trans. Helen R. Lane (New York: Harcourt Brace Jovanovich, 1985), 7.

13. Items 26–35 are taken from Ruth Leger Sivard, *World Military and Social Expenditures 1986* (Washington, D.C.: World Priorities, 1986), 47.

14. See Theodore Roszak, *Person/Planet: The Creative Disintegration of Industrial Society* (Garden City, N.Y.: Doubleday, 1978), xxvii.

15. Ibid., xxx.

16. See George Konrad, *Antipolitics*, trans. Richard E. Allen (New York: Harcourt Brace Jovanovich, 1984), 12.

17. In discussing such recognition, we should recall Unamuno's "man of flesh and bone . . . the man who is born, suffers and dies—above all, who dies; the man who eats and drinks and plays and sleeps and thinks and wills; the man who is seen and heard; the brother, the real brother."

2

The United States and South Africa

"I N our time," wrote Thomas Mann, "the destiny of man presents its meaning in political terms." Nowhere is this more obvious than in the idea of constructive engagement. An expression of almost unparalleled gall, this policy has revealed America's closed universe of understanding, a universe that draws comfort from endless humiliations. The final victims of constructive engagement will not be the black subjects of South Africa—for the days of their captivity are numbered—but all the people of the United States. Long after South Africa has thrown off the yoke of apartheid, the United States may remain in servitude (if it has not been annihilated by nuclear war), imprisoned not by the absence of political freedoms but by unreason and dishonor.

Constructive engagement did not fail. To offer such a judgment would presume that it was intended to succeed. The purpose of constructive engagement was to make monstrosity palatable, to allow Americans to support barbarism without suffering pangs of conscience or remorse. Described as an effort to seek deliverance "behind the scenes," it was never more than a scheme to keep up the struggle against the Soviet Union. Spawned by the same twisted reflexes that market impossible dreams through commercial advertising, it used human rights only as subterfuge.

With its policy of constructive engagement America saw itself as the misunderstood mentor of a benighted black population, one that was simply too backward to recognize its own interests. In the words of Oliver Tambo, president of the African National Congress (ANC) and chairman of its Political-Military Council: "Today, still the infantile dwarfs of yore, unable to think for ourselves, inanimate fruit ready for the picking by whosoever has sufficient strength to rule the garden patch, we are being taken under the protective wing of the United States, to save us from falling victim to an alleged communist expansionism."[1]

As with any nefarious doctrine, constructive engagement had its theoreticians. Some of these were merely fools, contemporary incarnations of Voltaire's professor of "metaphysico-theologo-cosmolonigology," whose incapacity for serious thought led them to preposterous rationalizations of scandal. "It is demonstrable," said Dr. Pangloss, "that things cannot be otherwise than they are: for all things having been made for some end, they must necessarily be for the best end." Others were genuinely insipid, dignifying calumny for the sake of privilege.

Whatever their motives, the theoreticians of constructive engagement created disjunction between language and reality. This was not a new development. The idea of language as a vicious circle signifying nothing beyond itself was discussed by Nietzsche. And Wittgenstein, observing the regressive effects of language, commented: "Philosophy is a battle against bewitchment of our intelligence by the means of language."

But constructive engagement was not entirely an exercise in deception. If that were the case, the American public might have believed the administration's shallow cries of concern about freedom in South Africa. And the American public knew better.

Significantly, the president's willingness to overlook massive deprivations of human rights in South Africa drew on tacit popular support. Convinced that the contest between the United States and the Soviet Union overrides all other considerations of international relations, Americans have historically been prepared to tolerate apartheid as the "lesser evil." The fact that such tolerance contradicts both the American political tradition and the fundamental principles of international law[2] creates no special difficulties. After all, virtually no one understands this tradition or recognizes these principles.

Evil, as we learn from Hannah Arendt, can be "banal."[3] It can be the product not only of brutishness and malevolence but of thoughtlessness. By this we mean not a lack of caring or compassion, but rather a literal absence of thought.

With respect to issues of foreign affairs the American public—as a herd—does not really think. Tantalized by exaggerated claims of national primacy and power, it sanctions every policy that promises to keep us "Number One." As a result, the United States now finds itself opposed from without by friends and foes alike.

In an interview during the German book fair in New York in March 1983, Günter Grass spoke of a "deficient knowledge" in this country that has become "ominous." Rejecting America's pretensions to be the bearer of an advanced civilization, Grass lamented the profound "ignorance of a world power in regard to the world." Noting that "the lack of readiness of the general public, even among the educated classes in the United States, really to become more familiar with other cultures" is nothing less than a threat to American survival, Grass warned of the need for expanded awareness. "Otherwise," he insisted, "as already in Vietnam and soon in Central America or in another place, they will encounter their next disastrous defeats."[4]

Günter Grass was correct. There has been no learning from lessons of the past. With its policies in South Africa (Grass's "another place") the Reagan administration has repeated the persistent failures of earlier policies. Vitalized by a flawed understanding of power politics, the United States may even continue to subject entire populations of the powerless to murder and infamy. This will be the true legacy of constructive engagement. This will be the only outcome of "silent diplomacy."

In the not-too-distant future apartheid will be overthrown, creating a successor black government with prominently anti-American leanings. When this happens, Americans will once again discover that ceaseless deference to thoughtlessness is always unrealistic. In the fashion of other revolutionary governments spawned by reaction to U.S.–supported repressive regimes, the new black government of South Africa will join the expanding legion of anti-American states.

How will the United States respond? The answer is highly predictable. This country will begin the next phase of geopolitical struggle, mounting an active insurgency against the new regime. Resembling the Reagan administration's curious war against Nicaragua, this insurgency—conducted by "freedom fighters"—will seek to topple a "Soviet pawn."

Violence is not power. Sometimes they are opposites. To sustain

both its interests and its ideals, the United States must begin to acknowledge justice as the only pragmatic standard of its policy toward
South Africa.

By making anti-Sovietism the centerpiece of its foreign policy,
the Reagan administration accepts a pernicious doctrine that might
makes right. Standing by a regime in Pretoria that is founded on
organized slavery and murder (little has been changed by sanctions),
this country rejects both the higher-law bases of the American political tradition and the fundamental rules of modern international law.
A series of libels camouflaged as patriotism, the administration's
apologetics on South Africa now represent the acme of this bilious
genre in world affairs.

How strange it is! America, a country born in revolution, has
become the most counterrevolutionary country on earth. America, a
country that is based on the principle of "just cause" for revolution,
still effectively opposes the right of millions of oppressed black South
Africans to struggle for the right to "life, liberty and the pursuit of
happiness." As Oliver Tambo observes: "Countries which are proud
of the armed revolutions which brought their peoples democracy are,
because of their support for the racists, equally fervent in their de-
nunciation of our armed combatants as terrorists."[5]

In a century where fantasies of the infernal have become history,
there is little evidence of improved vision in the United States.
Rather than embark on a course of decency and promise, the Reagan
administration chooses to cling to a cosmetically improved program
of "gentle persuasion." For all who cherish the idea of America as a
beacon light to a drowning world, the gentleness is terrifying.

Gentleness cannot overcome racism. And apartheid is an insti-
tutionalized form of racism. In the words of Oliver Tambo:

> Racism, the theory and practice of the domination of one race by
> another, and specifically its apartheid expression, cannot be re-
> formed. Like Nazism, its antecedent and sister crime against hu-
> manity, it must be overthrown and uprooted forcibly, in its totality.
> Those who argue to the contrary and even claim that the Pretoria
> regime has embarked on reform, are either grossly misled or are
> bent on protecting the regime of racial tyranny by seeking to re-
> furbish its image to make it more acceptable. In any case, a cancer
> cannot be its own cure. The fanatical racists who have spent more

than half-a-century drawing up the blueprints of the apartheid system and transforming those theoretical constructions into the South African society we know today, cannot, at the same time, be the agents for the abolition of that system.[6]

The Reagan administration does not intend to do evil with its retrograde policy on South Africa. The administration believes that it supports one form of evil for the sake of a greater good. Expressed in the desolate syntax of the cold war, this means that apartheid is admittedly wrong, but that the alternative—expanded Soviet influence in southern Africa—is even worse.

Leaving aside the inherently spurious nature of any such comparison, this calculation is all wrong. The prospect of increased Soviet influence over South Africa is *enlarged* by policies of constructive engagement. To preserve South Africa as an ally, the United States must stand firmly against the Botha regime. Although it is already very late to expect black support in that country, there is no other way. Goodness and geopolitical interest coincide.

Further, goodness cannot coexist with large-scale human sacrifices to abstract ideals. If the cost of opposing Soviet influence around the world were the death and degradation of millions of innocents, that cost would be unacceptable. The ends do not justify the means. Indeed, the very idea of an improved world order derived from human suffering is a travesty of reasoning, a rhetorical manipulation that transports us all to the outer limits of sanity and despair.

What sort of suffering do we observe in South Africa? Consider the following:[7]

Over 20,000 antiapartheid activists, including children as young as seven years old, have been summarily jailed by the regime. Under the catch-all "law" of "public violence," many have been tortured; several have been killed. Another regulation makes it a crime for journalists to *witness* antiapartheid protests, as well as to report on their activities.

White South Africans, representing 18 percent of the population, own 87 percent of the land. Black people who are "unfit to work" are confined to ten "homelands," dividing families as workers travel hundreds of miles to the townships. The homelands have been carved by the apartheid regime from the state's poorest land.

Each white community is paired with a black township (a ghetto) where black workers must stay each night. Each morning they enter the white communities to work in twelve hour shifts for as little as $2. White South Africans, on the other hand, enjoy one of the world's most affluent life styles.

Every year South Africa exports over a billion dollars worth of food products, and every day an average of 136 black children in South Africa die of malnutrition.

In a nation with one of the most advanced medical-care systems in the world, one in four black South African babies dies at birth; one in two by the age of five.

With its policy of constructive engagement, the Reagan administration has operated against reason, against life. Informed American citizens must take the initiative to reverse this policy before it is too late. The president can never be expected to move forward on his own or even with congressional prodding. Anesthetized to understanding, he will respond only to a newly conscious vanguard of the electorate. This vanguard must ground its arguments in the finest traditions of both the American polity and the essential norms of international law.

The American Political Tradition

The idea of a higher law figured importantly in the creation of the United States. Codified in both the Declaration of Independence and in the Constitution, this idea rests on the acceptance of certain principles of right and justice that obtain because of their own obvious merit. Such principles, as Sir William Blackstone declared, are nothing less than "the eternal, immutable laws of good and evil, to which the creator himself in all his dispensations conforms; and which he has enabled human reason to discover so far as they are necessary for the conduct of human actions."

When Jefferson drafted the Declaration he drew freely on Aristotle, Cicero, Grotius, Vattel, Pufendorf, Burlamaqui, and Locke's

Second Treatise of Government. Asserting the right of revolution whenever government becomes destructive of "certain unalienable rights," the Declaration of Independence posits a natural world order whose laws are external to all human will and are discoverable through human reason. Although by the eighteenth century God had withdrawn from immediate contact with humankind and had been transformed into final cause or prime mover of the universe, nature provided an appropriate substitute. Through the decisive influence of Isaac Newton, whose *Principia* was first published in 1686, all of creation could be taken as an expression of divine will. The only way to know God's will was to discover the law of nature; Locke and Jefferson deified nature and denatured God.

What exactly was this law of nature? As Jefferson learned from Locke, it was the law of reason. According to Locke's second treatise:

> The state of nature has a law to govern it, which obliges every one: and *reason, which is that law,* teaches all mankind, who will but consult it, that being all equal and independent, no one ought to harm another in his life, health, liberty, or possessions. . . . In transgressing the law of nature, the offender declares himself to live by another rule than that of *reason and common equity, which is that measure God has set to the actions of men.* . . . A criminal, who having renounced *reason, the common rule and measure God hath given to mankind,* hath, by the unjust violence and slaughter he hath committed on one, declared war against all mankind.

As reason is the only sure guide to what God has given humankind, reason is the only foundation of true law. This Lockean and Jeffersonian idea of a transcendent or higher law is expressed not only in the Declaration of Independence but in the Constitution. The Ninth Amendment, in stipulating that "the enumeration of certain rights in this Constitution shall not prejudice other rights not so enumerated," reflects the belief in a law superior to the will of human governance. This belief runs continuously from ancient times to the present.

The fragments of Heraclitus attest to the antiquity of the idea of a higher law: "For all human laws are nourished by one, which is divine. For it governs as far as it will, and is sufficient for all, and more than enough." Such Heraclitean dicta, offered somewhere around 500 B.C., entered into later Stoic philosophy, describing one universal and rational law.

In 442 B.C. Sophocles elucidated the idea of true law as an act of discovery, challenging the superiority of human rule making in *Antigone*. Exploring the essential conflict between claims of the state and the individual conscience, this drama has since been taken to represent the incontestable supremacy of a higher law over man-made law. In the nineteenth century Thoreau, noting that men live with "too passive a regard for the moral laws," cited *Antigone* as a stirring example of civil disobedience.

Building upon Plato's theory of Ideas, which sought to elevate nature from the realm of contingent facts to the realm of immutable archetypes or Forms, Aristotle advanced in his *Ethics* the concept of "natural justice." Quoting *Antigone*, he argued that "an unjust law is not a law." This position, of course, is in stark contrast to the opinion of the Sophists that justice is never more than an expression of supremacy, that it is what Thrasymachus, in Plato's *Republic*, calls "the interest of the stronger."

The Stoics, whose legal philosophy arose on the threshold of the Greek and Roman worlds, regarded nature itself as the supreme legislator in the moral order. Applying Platonic and Aristotelian thought to the emerging cosmopolis, they defined this order as one in which humankind, through its divinely granted capacity to reason, can commune directly with the gods. Since this definition required an expansion of Plato's and Aristotle's developing notions of universalism, the Stoics articulated a division between *lex aeterna, ius natural*, and *ius humanum* (eternal law, natural law, and man-made law).

Lex aeterna is the law of reason of the cosmos, the Logos that rules the universe. As an emanation of cosmic reason, human reason rules the lives of men. Natural law partakes of eternal law, though it has a more limited range of application. Unlike the more elitist conception of Plato (and to a certain extent Aristotle), the Stoic idea of an innate right reason presumed no divisions between peoples. Rather, in linking all persons with the cosmic order, it established the essential foundations of true universality.

Cicero in *De Republica* defined the state as a "coming together of a considerable number of men who are united by a common agreement about law and rights and by the desire to participate in mutual advantages." This definition sheds light on the problems surrounding positivist jurisprudence, a legal philosophy that values a state's edicts as intrinsically just and obligatory. In a famous passage of *De Republica*, Cicero sets forth the classic statement on natural law:

> True law is right reason, harmonious with nature, diffused among all, constant, eternal; a law which calls to duty by its commands and restrains from evil by its prohibitions. . . . It is a sacred obligation not to attempt to legislate in contradiction to this law; nor may it be derogated from nor abrogated. Indeed, by neither the Senate nor the people can we be released from this law; nor does it require any but oneself to be its expositor or interpreter. Nor is it one law at Rome and another at Athens; one now and another at a late time; but one eternal and unchangeable law binding all nations through all time.

What is to be done when man-made law varies from true law? The Romans incorporated in their statutes a contingency clause stating that man-made law could never abrogate sacred obligations. On several occasions Cicero and others invoked this clause, or *jus*, against one statute or another. The written law of the moment, never more than an artifact of the civic community, remained subject to right reason.

Later St. Augustine reaffirmed that temporal law must conform to the unchangeable eternal law, which he defined as "the reason or will of God" (*ratio divina vel voluntas Dei*). Aquinas continued this tradition of denying the status of law to prescriptions that are unjust (*lex iniusta non est lex*). "Human law," he wrote in the *Summae*, "has the quality of law only insofar as it proceeds according to right reason; and in this respect it is clear that it derives from the eternal law. Insofar as it deviates from reason it is called an unjust law, and has the quality not of law, but of violence."

The concept of a higher law was widely integrated into medieval jurisprudential thought. According to John of Salisbury's *Policraticus*, "there are certain precepts of the law which have perpetual necessity, having the force of law among all nations and which absolutely cannot be broken." Recognizing the idea that all political authority must be intrinsically limited, John noted that the prince "may not lawfully have any will of his own apart from that which the law or equity enjoins, or the calculation of the common interest requires." Natural law, then, exists to frustrate political injustice.

In the seventeenth and eighteenth centuries natural law doctrine was reaffirmed and secularized by Grotius. Reviving the Ciceronian idea of natural law and its underlying optimism about human nature, Grotius liberated this idea from any remaining dependence on ecclesiastical or papal interpretation. Building on the speculations of the Dominican Francisco de Vitoria, who had proclaimed a natural community of humankind and the universal validity of human rights, Grotius fashioned a bridge from the Christian *oecumene* of the Middle Ages to a new interstate society. He strengthened the idea of a universally valid natural law transcending in obligation all human law, including the law of the sovereign state.

Unlike Machiavelli and Hobbes, therefore, Grotius did not reduce law to the will of the prince or of the state. Rather, while recognizing such will as a constitutive element in the international legal order, he believed that the binding quality of human edicts must be derived from the overriding totality of natural imperatives. Hence he proceeded to reject *raison d'état* as a just cause for war.

This brings us to the transmittal of natural law ideas into American political theory, a transmittal that was preeminently through the *Second Treatise* of Locke (1690). The codified American "duty" to revolt when governments commit "a long train of abuses and usurpations" flows from Locke's notion that civil authority can never extend beyond the securing of humankind's natural rights. Significantly, the motto that Jefferson chose for his seal was "Rebellion to Tyrants Is Obedience to God." As for the right to pursue happiness, which Jefferson drew from Burlamaqui's incorporation into natural law, it had nothing whatever to do with today's contemporary celebrations of materialism. Rather, Jefferson viewed happiness (in deference to Pufendorf and Locke) as a condition to be achieved through commitment to reason.

Above all else, perhaps, the Declaration of Independence codified a social contract that sets limits on the power of *any* government. Its purpose was to articulate a set of universally valid constraints on all secular political authority. As justice, which is based on natural law, binds all human society, the rights described by the Declaration of Independence cannot be reserved only to Americans. They extend to all societies and can never be abrogated by man-made law.

This theory of a higher law is based on clarity, self-evidence, and coherence. Its validity cannot be shaken by the presumed imperatives of geopolitics, even when Americans feel themselves threatened by an Evil Empire. To ignore the Declaration of Independence in the making of U.S. foreign policy is illogical and self-contradictory, because it nullifies the immutable and universal law of nature from which the Declaration derives.

To act against the principles of the Declaration of Independence is to act against the permanent jurisprudential foundations of the United States, foundations grounded in natural law. No exhortations of current danger can or should require us, as Americans, to set aside these principles. As noted by the Swiss scholar Emmerich de Vattel in the 1758 edition of *The Law of Nations* (a work in which several American fathers of independence discovered important maxims of political liberty): "No agreement can bind, or even authorize, a man to violate the natural law." Rather, Vattel cautioned that only obedience to higher legal obligations can produce a virtuous and thus a safe and prosperous state: "One would have to be very ignorant of political affairs not to perceive how much more capable a virtuous Nation is of forming a happy, peaceful, flourishing and secure state, respected by its neighbors and formidable to its enemies."

This brings us back to the individual. In the end, the higher-law expectations of the American political tradition are not self-enforcing. Defied again and again by transient political elites, they can be sustained only where individuals seize their own inwardness and act (as does Antigone before Creon) according to conscience. "Why has every man a conscience?" asks Thoreau in his essay on *Civil Disobedience*: "I think that we should be men first, and subjects afterwards. It is not desirable to cultivate a respect for the law, so much as for the right. The only obligation which I have a right to assume is to do at any time what I think right. It is truly enough said that a corporation has no conscience; but a corporation of conscientious men is a corporation *with* a conscience."

Where are such conscientious men and women to be found? Certainly not, says Thoreau, among the "commonly esteemed good citizens." These mass men and women serve the state "not as men mainly, but as machines, with their bodies." Placing themselves "on a level with wood and earth and stones," they are incapable of making America's essential moral distinctions; thus, "they are as likely to serve the devil, without *intending* it, as God."

Can we create the conditions for a conscientious "corporation" through education of the citizenry? From Rousseau to the present, this has been the path of virtually all democratic theory. Rousseau believed that law and liberty could exist in a city-state of properly educated voters like Geneva. As he stipulates in book 3 of the *Social Contract*, that state must meet certain conditions: "First, a very small state where people can be readily got together and where each citizen can with ease know all the rest; secondly, great simplicity of manners, to prevent business from multiplying and raising thorny problems; next, a large measure of equality in rank and fortune, without which equality of rights and authority cannot long subsist; lastly little or no luxury—for luxury either comes of riches or makes them necessary."

The United States is far from meeting these conditions, and Rousseau's idea that (even under very definite conditions) a majority can be trusted with what is really best for "the people" is always baneful. The dangers of the general will have been made manifest not only in the exploits of Robespierre and Napoleon but also in the banal collectivism of contemporary America. What is required today in the United States is not that we should be "forced to be free" (Rousseau's imperative in the *Social Contract*) but that we should grasp our existing political freedoms and become persons. We require not the "noble savage" of Rousseau but the "civil savage," a construction of political philosopher Michael A. Weinstein, who describes "the masterless man," the one who seeks completion not in the other but in himself; the one who rejects the "predatory-parasitical lust" of contemporary politics and who dares not to acquiesce.

Rousseau's deification of the herd points toward the very opposite of the higher-law traditions of the United States. The Genevan made the People sovereign; for us, sovereignty must reside in the Person. As Thoreau understood, apathy, complacency, passivity, and moral cowardice are the inevitable trappings of the majority. Hope lies only in those whose primary allegience is to overriding and universal laws, not in the "good citizen" but in the "wise minority."

What is the task of this wise minority, of these few individuals whose choice of inwardness compels them to remain forever outside the grazing herd? Thoreau speaks of civil disobedience, an act of "counter-friction" that may undermine expediency and restore higher standards of personal judgment. Confronted with an evil of the sort Americans now confront, the evil of constructive engagement, Thoreau would urge, as he did in *Civil Disobedience* about other policy deformations, "Let your life be a counter-friction to stop the machine. What I have to do is to see, at any rate, that I do not lend myself to the wrong which I condemn."

Even Thoreau's prescription, however, is inadequate. We also require self-liberation. For the United States to return to its own higher-law traditions, it will first have to end its obsessive anti-Sovietism. Before this can happen, American society itself will need to be transformed.

As we learn from Goethe, we depend on creatures of our own making. At the moment the creatures who speak for the United States lack even the remotest familiarity with American political tradition. Despite ritualized deference for the spirit of democracy, these creatures positively glow with nostalgia for anciens régimes, distancing themselves from calumny in a bouffant fantasy of antidemocratic pomp. In the Reaganite political culture, the administration removes the "safety net" of essential services from the disadvantaged while the inner circle sensationalizes its own prosperity. For the members of this circle, American indifference to repression in other lands is merely anecdotal, and natural law an assurance that privilege will not yield to thought. As for those who would seek more vigorous U.S. opposition to apartheid, let them eat cake.

The Rules of International Law

The Reagan administration's disdain for human rights in South Africa is more than an ironic break with our own revolutionary traditions. It is also a rejection of certain peremptory norms (*jus cogens*) of international law. While the break with tradition falls within the volitional ambit of states in world politics, the rejection of incontrovertible juridical standards does not. Rather, such rejection represents a breach of accepted rules and principles that endangers the entire edifice of civilized international relations.

The Nuremberg trials at the end of World War II created a revolution in international legal affairs. Among other things, this revolution essentially removed a state's treatment of its own nationals from the realm of domestic jurisdiction whenever such treatment fails to conform to particular normative standards. Expanding on the long-standing principle of humanitarian intervention, the Nuremberg Principles place additional and far-reaching limits on the authority of particular states. Reasoning that the individual human being, as the ultimate unit of all law, is entitled to the protection of humankind when the state tramples upon his or her rights "in a manner that outrages the conscience of mankind," the Nuremberg Tribunal firmly established the *obligation* of states to intervene in other states whenever such outrages are committed.

In the absence of viable community enforcement capabilities in our decentralized international society, a pattern of justice requires voluntary compliance and support by individual governments. The prevailing expectation is that such compliance will be especially accepted by the world's major powers. Punishment of gross violations of human rights is now well within the jurisdictional scope of U.S. foreign policy.

For the United States the Nuremberg obligations are in a sense doubly binding. They are not only international law but also the obligations of the American political tradition. By their codification of the principle that fundamental human rights are not an internal question for each state but an imperious postulate of the international community, the Nuremberg obligations are a point of convergence between the law of nations and the jurisprudential/ethical foundations of the American republic.

If the United States continues to turn its back on responsible enforcement of the international law of human rights, it will lose its few remaining claims to moral leadership and also its last practical chance for harmony with the developing world. Indeed, the Reagan administration's retrograde policy on human rights may soon lose this country its friends as well. The administration's problem lies in recognizing the principle of "just cause" for insurgency (a principle enshrined in our traditions and in the law of nations) and in distinguishing between lawful and unlawful insurgencies under international law.

What features of the international legal order explain the principle of just cause? Although world law has consistently condemned particular acts of international terrorism, it has also countenanced certain uses of force that derive from "the inalienable right to self-determination and independence of all peoples under colonial and racist regimes and other forms of alien domination and the legitimacy of their struggle, in particular the struggle of national liberation movements, in accordance with the purposes and principles of the Charter and the relevant resolutions of the organs of the United Nations." This exemption, from the 1973 General Assembly Report of the Ad Hoc Committee on International Terrorism, is corroborated by Article 7 of the UN General Assembly's 1974 Definition of Aggression.

Contemporary international law also codifies the right of insurgents to use certain levels and types of force when fundamental human rights are repressed (whether or not these rights include self-determination) and where nonviolent methods of redress are unavailable. Inhabiting a sovereignty-centered system in which the normative rules of human rights are normally not enforceable by central global institutions, the individual victims of human rights abuse must seek relief in appropriate forms of humanitarian assistance or intervention by sympathetic states and/or in approved forms of rebellion. Indeed, without such self-help remedies the protection of human rights in a decentralized legal setting would be entirely a fiction, assuring little more than the primacy of realpolitik.

As we have seen, current human rights law—which is spelled out in the UN Charter, the UN Universal Declaration of Human Rights (1948), the International Covenant on Civil and Political Rights (1976), and the International Covenant on Economic, Social and Cultural Rights (1976)—originated in ancient Greece and Rome. From Greek Stoicism and Roman law to the present, the *jus gentium* (law of nations) and modern international law have accepted the right of individuals to overthrow tyrants, forcefully if necessary. This acceptance can be found in international custom; the general principles of law recognized by nations; UN General Assembly resolutions; various judicial decisions; specific compacts and documents such as the Magna Carta (1215), the Petition of Right (1628), the English Bill of Rights (1689), the Declaration of Independence (1776), and the Declaration of the Rights of Man and of the Citizen (1789); the writings of highly qualified publicists such as Cicero, Francisco de Vitoria, Hugo Grotius, and Emmerich de Vattel; and, by extrapolation, in the absence of effective, authoritative institutions in world politics.

International law, therefore, actually supports the legitimacy of certain forms of insurgency. While this is important for the objectives of international justice, it does create severe problems in promoting the objectives of international order. The ultimate problem, of course, is allowing international law to serve the interests of order without impairing the legitimate interests of justice.

How are we to determine the proper balance? What criteria can be applied? Given the decentralized system of international law, individual states must bear the final responsibility for distinguishing between terrorism and lawful acts of insurgency.

What principles should inform their judgments? First, careful assessments must be made of particular regimes' conformance with the international law of human rights. Regime terror spawns revolutionary violence and must be opposed strenuously by the community of nations.

Second, states must exhibit a deep and abiding concern for discrimination and proportionality in evaluating the legitimacy of insurgent uses of force. Force applied to any segment of human population, blurring the distinction between combatants and noncombatants, is terrorism. Similarly, force applied to the fullest possible extent, restrained only by the limits of available weaponry, is terrorism.

In the words of the Report of the General Assembly's Ad Hoc Committee on International Terrorism (1973): "Even when the use of force is legally and morally justified, there are some means, as in every form of human conflict, which must not be used; the legitimacy of a cause does not in itself legitimatize the use of certain forms of violence, especially against the innocent." As in war between states, every use of force by insurgents must be judged twice; once with regard to the justness of the objective, and once with regard to the justness of the means used in the fighting.

The explicit application of codified restrictions of the law of war to noninternational armed conflicts dates back only as far as the four Geneva Conventions of 1949. However, as the laws of war, like the whole of international law, comprise more than treaties and conventions, it is clear that the obligations of *jus in bello* (justice in war) are part of the general principles of law recognized by civilized nations and are binding on *all* categories of belligerents. Indeed, the Hague Convention (No. IV) of 1907 declared in broad terms that in the absence of a precisely published set of guidelines in humanitarian international law concerning "unforseen cases," all belligerency is governed by all of the pre-conventional sources of international law: "Until a more complete code of the laws of war has been issued, the High Contracting Parties deem it expedient to declare that, in cases not included in the Regulations adopted by them, the inhabitants and the belligerents remain under the protection and the rule of the principles of the law of nations, as they result from the usages established among civilized peoples, from the laws of humanity, and the dictates of public conscience."

This "more complete code" became available with the adoption of the four Geneva Conventions on August 12, 1949. These agreements contained a common article (3) under which the convention provisions would be applicable in noninternational armed conflicts. Nevertheless, the 1949 Geneva Diplomatic Conference rejected the idea that all of the laws of war should apply to internal conflicts, and in 1970 the UN Secretary General requested that additional rules relating to noninternational armed conflicts be adopted in the form of a protocol or a separate convention.

In 1974 the Swiss government convened in Geneva the Diplomatic Conference on the Reaffirmation and Development of International Humanitarian Law Applicable in Armed Conflicts. On June 8, 1977, the conference formally adopted two protocols additional to the Geneva Conventions of 1949. Protocol II relates "to the Protection of Victims of Non-International Armed Conflicts" and develops and supplements common Article 3 of the 1949 Conventions. Although, in the fashion of common Article 3 and Article 19 of the 1954 Hague Cultural Property Convention, Protocol II does not apply to situations of internal disturbances and tensions such as riots or isolated and sporadic acts of violence, it does apply to all

armed conflicts "which take place in the territory of a High Contracting Party between its armed forces and dissident armed forces
or other organized armed groups which, under responsible command, exercise such control over a part of its territory and to enable
them to carry out sustained and concerted military operations and
to implement this Protocol."

Geneva Protocol I also constrains insurgent uses of force in
"armed conflicts in which people are fighting against colonial domination and alien occupation and against racist regimes in the exercise
of their right of self-determination." Thus, even where the peremptory rights to self-determination are being exercised, insurgent forces
must resort to lawful means of combat. According to Article 35,
which reaffirms long-standing norms of international law: "In any
armed conflict, the right of the Parties to the conflict to choose methods or means of warfare is not unlimited."

The American imperative must be to condemn not only insurgent terror, but also "regime" terror. Regime terror, which contradicts the rules and principles of international law, *breeds* insurgent
terror. If the United States is to be true to the basic ideals of its
founding documents as well as to its international legal obligations
and long-term geopolitical interests, it cannot continue to support
terrorist regimes while combating insurgents.

Who are the terrorists? According to South Africa's Terrorism
Act of 1967, terrorism is defined, inter alia, as any behavior that
embarrasses the regime or which would "cause, encourage or further
feelings of hostility between the White and other inhabitants of the
Republic." Is this a definition with which Americans can agree?

The South African constitution contains no Bill of Rights to protect the natural rights of the individual. Even under the best of circumstances, that is, without the special harshness of emergency
powers, police officers can arrest without warrant any person *suspected* of being a terrorist. Such a person may be held for interrogation for as long as it takes for the prisoner "to reply satisfactorily to
all questions of the said interrogation." In other words, a person may
be held until a carefully orchestrated pattern of beatings and torture
elicits the desired response.

Detainees can be held for more than a year without being formally charged. While under detention, an individual may receive no
visits from family, friends, clergy, or counsel. No right of habeas

corpus or recourse to the courts exists. To be found guilty under the Terrorism Act can mean a sentence of death.

Can we characterize the opponents of such a regime as terrorists? Faced with such a regime, can we reasonably expect the black leadership to renounce the use of force? Significantly, the Commonwealth Group on South Africa, also known as the Eminent Persons Group, in its report of June 12, 1986, explains that it is "neither possible nor reasonable to have people permanently forswear the only power available to them should the government walk away from the negotiating table. In a situation in which people have no rights and no participation in their government, ultimately they cannot be denied the right to take up arms."[8]

The government of South Africa is not prepared to negotiate. After meeting with the South African Cabinet Constitutional Committee on May 19, 1986, the Commonwealth Group concluded that the South African government is "not yet prepared to negotiate fundamental change, nor to countenance the creation of genuine democratic structures, nor to face the prospect of the end of white domination and white power in the forseeable future."[9]

On the basis of its evaluation of existing policies, the Commonwealth Group was unanimous in holding to the view that "a much greater descent into violence is inevitable." Yet, it also maintained that one remaining factor might prevent full-scale guerrilla warfare:

> There is only one factor remaining which might prevent that kind of destruction. If the major Western states that have trade weight with South Africa really seek to bring pressure to bear on the South African government, those decisions toward greater violence may be deferred and may even be made unnecessary. That pressure can be evidenced through sanctions. Without such actions, the view of black leaders that they are without fundamental support from the West will again be confirmed.[10]

In terms of constructive engagement, this finding means prompt and serious American disengagement from a discredited policy. As the Commonwealth Group concludes:

> Over the last five or six years, the two most powerful leaders in the free world—President Reagan and Prime Minister Thatcher—

have attempted, by diplomacy, by "constructive engagement," to achieve change. At that time, the condition of the blacks is worse than it was at the beginning of this approach because of the successive emergencies and the use of punitive powers. Why would anyone expect words alone to be successful tomorrow or next year?[11]

The United States must make very critical distinctions between terrorists and legitimate revolutionary movements. These distinctions must be based on more important criteria than those generated by anti-Sovietism. Even in narrow geopolitical terms, a continuing American retreat from human rights in foreign affairs will ultimately have devastating repercussions. In the not-too-distant future, our access to South Africa's vital mineral resources will depend upon the degree of our commitment to black majority rule.

In the aftermath of the Holocaust, the philosopher Karl Jaspers addressed the question of German guilt. His response articulates one of the most fertile and important concepts of modern thought, the idea of "metaphysical guilt." Jaspers wrote: "There exists a solidarity among men as human beings that makes each co-responsible for every wrong and every injustice in the world, especially for crimes committed in his presence or with his knowledge. If I fail to do whatever I can to prevent them, I too am guilty." Understood in terms of this country's current unconcern for ongoing crimes against humanity, Jaspers' doctrine suggests an urgent need to confront overriding Nuremberg obligations, a need that challenges us both individually and collectively to oppose such crimes while there is still time.

The Personal Imperative

"Everything in this world exudes crime," says Baudelaire, "the newspapers, the walls, and the face of man." Today this is nowhere more apparent than in South Africa, where the survival of millions has been expected to wait upon the rhythms of constructive engagement. The crime of South Africa thus lies not only in the fiber of local executioners but in the complicity of Americans. Existing as a futile parody of national traditions and international rules, this complicity creates a garden of evil without hope for escape. In the end, as we have noted, the victims will include not only multitudes of black South Africans but the entire United States.

This is the essential starting point of understanding, of lucidity that can produce change. Before Americans can press forward against apartheid, they will have to understand *themselves* as victims. It is initially for ourselves that we must oppose the ruthless exploitation underway in South Africa. This was understood by Steve Biko, who wrote in 1972 (five years before he was put into leg irons, tortured, and beaten to death by South African Security Police): "The liberals must fight on their own and for themselves. If they are true liberals they must realize that they themselves are oppressed, and that they must fight for their own freedom and not that of the blacks with whom they can hardly claim identification."[12]

Biko was speaking of white liberals in South Africa. But his wisdom applies equally well to conscious people elsewhere. It is the key to effective transformation of apartheid and ultimately to hope for America.

How shall we proceed? Recognizing the difference between law and right (and therefore the higher law principles of this nation), Henry David Thoreau counseled civic responsibility to oppose unjust foreign policies. To seize the present moment as Thoreau would have advised, Americans need do no more than act according to their own best traditions. Returning to that original spirit championed by Jefferson and Paine as well as Locke and Thoreau, they need only understand that true patriotism must be directed not toward current leaders but to underlying and incontrovertible principles.

Faced with stark intimations of their complicity in the crimes of constructive engagement, individual Americans must now demand a change of direction from Washington. Recalling the promising visions of the Declaration of Independence, they must build on the understanding that thoughtless submission to governmental authority is the ethos not of democracy but of despotism. The appropriate model of the responsible patriot in contemporary American life must no longer be the deferential private citizen who fears to think (the cherished model of the Reagan administration), but rather one who rejects this fear as a betrayal of American political traditions—a betrayal that is a thinly disguised and ultimately lethal form of servitude.

In choosing to challenge the Reagan administration on constructive engagement, the American patriot also acts in compliance with the judicial structure of global accountability established at Nuremberg. This may be the case even where personal challenges involve the violation of specific domestic laws. Indeed, since resisting crimes of state is the overriding legal duty stipulated by the Nuremberg Principles, the true lawbreakers are not individual opponents of apartheid (for example, American citizens who are arrested for protesting in front of the South African embassy in Washington), but rather the leaders of the United States that sustain an odious regime.

For a related example, consider the Sanctuary movement now operating in the United States. Opposing their government's crimes in El Salvador and Guatemala (crimes, as in South Africa, that involve support of authoritarian governments for presumed geopolitical advantage), these Americans are arrested as "criminals" for rescuing Central American refugees from torture and death. Though based on predominantly religious principles of sanctuary, these 50,000 Americans of every faith act in support of the overriding obligations of international law. The lawbreakers are not these Americans who oppose the Reagan administration's classification of Salvadorans and Guatemalans as economic rather than political refugees (because they have fled from reactionary anti-Soviet oligarchies supported by the United States), but an American leadership elite that sends tens of thousands of innocent civilians to be murdered in their countries as the presumed cost of competition in the cold war.

In the years before the Civil War thousands of Americans organized an Underground Railroad to help those fleeing from slavery. At that time, those who participated in this movement were judged lawbreakers by the federal government and were frequently imprisoned under the Fugitive Slave Act. Today it is widely recognized that the only lawbreakers of the period were those who sustained the system of slavery, and that every individual act to oppose this system was genuinely law enforcing. Similar patterns of recognition will soon emerge in regard to the Sanctuary movement, but not, alas, until the Reagan administration has further profaned the image of America as a refuge from persecution.

We live at the margins of history. Heavy with the burdens of inconscience, we have learned to love paradox, content with a foreign policy that opposes the most sacred foundations of American political life. Unable to rise even to indignation, we take refuge in clichés, pretending that our leaders know best and that even crimes against humanity have their proper place.

Once such crimes were infamous. Yesterday we put them on trial. Today they are rationalized.

We know what must be done. But we persist in gestures that will ensure failure, gestures that remind one of the would-be rescuer's exhortations in Camus's *The Fall*: "Oh young woman, throw yourself into the water again so that I may a second time have the chance of saving both of us. A second time, eh, what a risky suggestion! Just suppose, *cher maitre*, that we should be taken literally? We'd have to go through with it. Burr. . . ! The water's so cold! But let's not worry! It's too late now. It will always be too late. Fortunately!"

It need not be too late. There is another way. Without laying claim to innocence (that is no longer possible), we may challenge the wizardry of constructive engagement. Reaffirming our faith in American political institutions and in the complementary norms of international law, we may dissent when crimes of state don the apparel of geopolitical necessity. Anguished by slave camps identified as part of the "free world" and by massacres compelled by competition with an Evil Empire, we must demand an end to "Newspeak" and a return to reason. Only this will serve life and reduce culpability.

But as we have already seen, such demands cannot be spawned by our present society. Gertrude Stein once told Ernest Hemingway, "You are all a *génération perdue*." We confront in America today not a lost generation but a lost nation, one whose failures and incapacities appear in young and old alike and show no signs of disappearing.

We mistake tranquility for satisfaction and potency. What do we gain if the very tranquility we celebrate is a source of our misfortune? "Tranquility," Rousseau says in *The Social Contract*, "is found also in dungeons; but is that enough to make them desirable places to live in? The Greeks imprisoned in the cave of the Cyclops lived there very tranquilly, while they were awaiting their turn to be devoured."

Before we can demand an end to America's policy toward South Africa, Americans will need to be less tranquil. This, in turn, requires a society wherein the universal need for affect can be satisfied outside the herd, outside the state that is consumed in a death struggle with another state. This kind of society will appear only if already conscious individuals display great courage and if substantial numbers of others can learn to seek worth within themselves. The final task is to understand the linkages between our reflections and our foreign policies. Recognizing that our prefabricated images reinforce a society bent on degrading and destroying itself, we must learn to be terrified by mirrors.

Notes

1. See Oliver Tambo, "Racism, Apartheid and a New World Order," *Third World Quarterly* 8, no. 3 (July 1986), xvii. This is an address delivered when Tambo received the Third World Prize for 1985 on behalf of Nelson Rolihahla Mandela and Nomzamo Winnie Mandela. Having become a member of the ANC National Executive in 1949, Tambo held successive posts in the organization and was charged with high treason in 1956. Subject to a series of banning orders, he was in 1960 directed by the ANC National Executive to leave the country and to continue to mobilize international support against apartheid while in exile.

2. On the particular crime of apartheid, see International Convention on the Suppression and Punishment of the Crime of Apartheid, *entered into force*, July 18, 1976, G.A. Res. 3068, 28 U.N. G.A.O.R., Supp. (No. 30), U.N. Doc. A/9030 (1974). See also International Convention on the Elimination of All Forms of Racial Discrimination, *entered into force*, Jan. 4, 1969, G.A. Res. 2160 A, 20 U.N. G.A.O.R., Supp. (No. 14), U.N. Doc. A/6014 (1966). Apartheid has been linked to genocide in the International Convention on the Suppression and Punishment of the Crime of Apartheid, and several efforts have been undertaken to make the practice of apartheid punishable under the terms of the Genocide Convention (see Convention on the Prevention and Punishment of the Crime of Genocide, *entered into force*, January 12, 1951). Moreover, in the Convention on the Non-Applicability of Statutory Limitations to War Crimes and Crimes Against Humanity, "inhuman acts resulting from the policy of apartheid" are qualified as "crimes against humanity." And in various UN documents, apartheid is associated with both genocide and crimes against humanity (see, for example, G.A. Res. 2545, XXIV, December 11, 1969; and G.A. Res. 2438, XXIII, December 19, 1968).

3. See Hannah Arendt, *Eichmann in Jerusalem: A Report on the Banality of Evil* (New York: Penguin, 1963).

4. See "The German Literary Supplement," *New York Times Book Review*, February 27, 1983, 2.

5. See Tambo, "Racism, Apartheid and a New World Order," xix.

6. Ibid., xviii.

7. Statistics are taken from studies by Grassroots International, a U.S.-based organization seeking to end apartheid without violence.

8. See Malcolm Fraser and Olusegun Obasanjo, "What To Do about South Africa," *Foreign Affairs* 65, no. 1 (Fall 1986), 156. At its October 1985 summit in Nassau, the 49-member Commonwealth decided "to establish a small group of eminent Commonwealth persons" that would seek to encourage the process of political dialogue in South Africa. The mandate of this Eminent Persons Group (EPG), as it became known, was set out in the Commonwealth Accord on Southern Africa, or the Nassau Accord. This accord called on the government of South Africa, inter alia, to "initiate in the context of a suspension of violence on all sides, a process of dialogue across lines of colour, politics and religion, with a view to establishing a non-racial and representative government." Over the course of six months, members of the group met with many members of the government and with virtually all the significant leaders of the black population, including Nelson Mandela. The EPG members were appointed by seven Commonwealth leaders and by Secretary-General Shridath S. Ramphal.

9. See Fraser and Obasanjo, "What To Do about South Africa," 155.

10. Ibid., 157.

11. Ibid., 158.

12. This comment appeared in 1972 in a volume, later banned, called *Student Perspectives on South Africa*, ed. H. W. van der Merwe and David Welsh in association with the Bailey Institute of Interracial Studies; reprinted in Donald Woods, *Biko* (New York and London: Paddington Press, 1978), 51.

3

The United States and Central America

S INCE the middle of the nineteenth century the United States has maintained hegemony over Central America. Today this region remains blocked from its aspirations, serving not its own particular needs and expectations but the purposes of a superpower. To a significant extent the failures of U.S. foreign policy in Central America can be described in terms of the issues of self-determination and nonintervention. These are issues of contemporary international law.

Among the norms of international law none is more important than nonintervention. Forming the basis for peaceful and productive relations among states, this norm is the touchstone of a civilized world order. Although, as we shall see, it is not absolute, the obligation of states to respect each other's sovereignty and independence is far-reaching. The right to intervene cannot derive from ideological distaste or from vague intimations of expected threats.

In its relations with Nicaragua, however, the United States ignores the territorial integrity and political independence of another nation without legal justification. Driven by antipathy for a Marxist regime in this hemisphere, the United States subordinates the rule of the law to the presumed imperatives of geopolitics. Invoking the rhetoric of freedom and democracy, the United States provides direct assistance to terrorist groups that would restore an earlier form of oligarchy.[1]

This lawless intervention in the internal affairs of Nicaragua[2] will prove counterproductive to the interests of the United States. During the next several years the contra rebels will be defeated, and the Sandinista regime will solidify its control of the country. At the same time, more and more states in the region will look upon the United States as an affliction, one that threatens their status as full members of the community of nations. Moreover, U.S. interventionism enlarges the prospect of nuclear war by heightening the chances for confrontation with the Soviet Union. By its support of the contras, for example, the United States moves toward a transnational civil war, with its client authoritarian regimes and counterrevolutionary forces fighting against leftist insurgents and revolutionary regimes backed by the Soviet Union.

Consider what happened late in 1986, after Congress approved $100 million in additional aid for the contras. Calling such approval a declaration of war—a reasonable call, to be sure, in the wake of the International Court of Justice (ICJ) decision of June 27, 1986—the Sandinista government responded by accelerating its buildup of armed forces and new weapons. In August 1986 the Nicaraguan army began drafting thousands of men, while the air force enlarged its fleet of Soviet-made helicopters. Honduras became a battleground as it allowed contra terrorists to operate on its territory in exchange for massive increases in U.S. military aid.

Unless foreign intervention is an indispensable corrective to gross violations of human rights, most texts and treatises on international law (an authoritative source of international law according to Article 38 of the Statute of the International Court of Justice) have long held that a state is forbidden to engage in military or paramilitary operations against another state with which it is not at war. Today, the long-standing customary prohibition against foreign support for lawless insurgencies is codified in the UN Charter and in the authoritative interpretation of that multilateral treaty at Article 1 and Article 3(g) of the 1974 UN General Assembly Definition of Aggression.

The legal systems embodied in the constitutions of individual states are an interest that all states must defend against aggression. This peremptory principle was expressed by Hersch Lauterpacht, who wrote concerning the scope of state responsibility for preventing acts of insurgency or terrorism against other states: "International law imposes upon the State the duty of restraining persons within its territory from engaging in such revolutionary activities against friendly States as amount to organized acts of force in the form of hostile expeditions against the territory of those States. It also obliges the States to repress and discourage activities in which attempts against the life of political opponents are regarded as a proper means of revolutionary action."[3]

Lauterpacht's rule reaffirms the Resolution on the Rights and Duties of Foreign Powers as Regards the Established and Recognized Governments in Case of Insurrection adopted by the Institute of International Law in 1900. His rule, however, stops short of the prescription offered by the eighteenth century Swiss scholar, Emmerich de Vattel. According to book 2 of Vattel's *The Law of Nations*, states that support wrongful insurgency directed at other states become the lawful prey of the world community: "If there should be found a restless and unprincipled nation, ever ready to do harm to others, to thwart their purposes, and to stir up civil strife among their citizens, there is no doubt that all others would have the right to unite together to subdue such a nation, to discipline it, and even to disable it from doing further harm."

Intervention is not always forbidden. Although as part of the international legal order individual governments are an interest that all states must defend against attack or foreign-directed subversion, this obligation may be reversed wherever particular governments act to disfigure human rights. Indeed, as we have already seen, since the Nuremberg trials and the end of World War II, a revolution in international legal affairs may permit states to intervene on behalf of insurgents within other states who are fighting against obvious regime terror. This revolution echoes E. Borchard's formulation in 1922:

Where a state under exceptional circumstances disregards certain rights of its own citizens, over whom presumably it has absolute sovereignty, the other states of the family of nations are authorized by international law to intervene on grounds of humanity. When the "human rights" are habitually violated, one or more states may intervene in the name of the society of nations and may take such measures as to substitute at least temporarily, if not permanently, its own sovereignty for that of the state thus controlled. Whatever the origin, therefore, of the rights of the individual, it seems as-

sured that these essential rights rest upon the ultimate sanction of
international law and will be protected, in last resort, by the most
appropriate organ of the international community.[4]

Borchard's formulation was prefigured by Hugo Grotius in book
2, chapter 25 of the seventeenth-century classic, *The Law of War and
Peace*:

> There is also another question, whether a war for the subjects of
> another be just, for the purpose of defending them from injuries
> inflicted by their ruler. Certainly it is undoubted that ever since
> civil societies were formed, the rulers of each claimed some special
> right over his subjects. Euripides makes his characters say that
> they are sufficient to right wrongs in their own city. And Thucy-
> dides puts among the marks of empire, the supreme authority in
> judicial proceedings. And so Virgil, Ovid and Euripides in the *Hip-
> polytus*. This is, as Ambrose says, that peoples may not run into
> wars by usurping the care for those who do not belong to them.
> The Corinthians in Thucydides say that it is right that each state
> should punish its own subjects. And Perseus says that he will not
> plead in defense of what he did against the Dolopians, since they
> were under his authority and he had acted upon his right. But all
> this applies when the subjects have really violated their duty; and
> we may add, when the case is doubtful. . . . But the case is differ-
> ent if the wrong be manifest. If a tyrant like Busiris, Phalaris,
> Diomede of Thrace practices atrocities toward his subjects, which
> no just man can approve, the right of human social connection is
> not cut off in such a case.

Human Rights in Central America

The U.S. argument that its actions against Nicaragua are motivated
by concern for human rights is transparently implausible. The contras—aided by their patrons in the United States—routinely commit
crimes of war and crimes against humanity. The America's Watch
report on human rights and U.S. policy in Latin America, *With
Friends Like These*, identifies a steady trail of "torture, massacres, indiscriminate aerial bombardment of civilians, systematic displace-
ment of peasants from their lands, the murder of children." In a

chapter titled "Geopolitics and Human Rights," the report states: "The fact is that the Fuerzas Democraticas Nicaraguenses, FDN [President Reagan's "freedom fighters," who are "the moral equal of the Founding Fathers"] has routinely attacked civilian populations. Their forces kidnap, torture, and murder health workers, teachers, and other government employees." Amnesty International in its annual report on human rights for 1986 describes "the routine practice of torture and summary execution by irregular forces opposing the Government of Nicaragua. . . . Opposition forces acting under the name *Unión Nacional de Oposición* (UNO), National Opposition Union, continued to routinely torture and summarily execute their captives. Some captives seized in border areas by UNO forces were removed to military base camps in Honduran territory. Amnesty International was concerned that torture and death threats were apparently tolerated by Honduran and United States officials advising and supplying UNO forces."

What else do we know about these terrorist groups, known collectively as the contras, and their supporters in the United States?

No one knows what they have done with funds that were transferred to their Swiss bank accounts in violation of the Boland Amendment, the Arms Export Act, the Neutrality Act, and other U.S. laws.

A twelve-page report on the contras, titled "Private Assistance and the Contras," prepared by Senator John F. Kerry in October 1986, describes "an interlocking web of bank accounts, air strips, planes, pilots and contra bases which have been used in common by weapon smugglers, narcotics smugglers, the contras and organizations assisting the contras."

Responding to the Massachusetts senator's investigation into illegal acts of support for the contras by the Reagan administration, Ambassador Robert E. White, a former U.S. ambassador to El Salvador and chairman of the Commission on United States–Central American Relations, discovered that:

The contras and their supporters in the United States were involved in the smuggling of drugs [apparently unwilling to accept Mrs. Reagan's advice to "just say no!"] to fund their war against Nicaragua.

The Federal Bureau of Investigation, the Office of the Attorney General, and the Department of Justice—when informed about these crimes—blocked all further investigation.

The contras and their supporters in the United States diverted congressional funds from humanitarian aid to guns and arms traffic.

Concern for human rights is clearly not a high priority of the U.S. government's contra war.

Further, the administration continues to support other regimes in the region beside which the Sandinistas compare quite favorably.[5] There is little cause to doubt that U.S. "covert" tactics are purely counterrevolutionary operations that deliberately subordinate humanitarian concerns to the presumed interest of geopolitics.

In Grenada the Reagan administration—faced with a threat from what the president described as "leftist thugs"—responded with a full-scale invasion.[6] In Guatemala, however, where almost a quarter of a million people have been exterminated during he past thirty years by a succession of military dictatorships, the administration favored the perpetrators of regime terror. Similar patterns of U.S. support are enjoyed by the Stroessner regime in Paraguay, which practices genocide against the Ache Indians under the seeing eyes of the American embassy in Asuncion, and by the Pinochet regime in Chile, which defiles essential human rights on an almost equally savage scale. Even after Pinochet's soldiers gleefully set fire to two university students as punishment for protest, Washington remained silent. Authoritarianism is freedom. Totalitarianism is tyranny. This is the Orwellian message of the Reagan administration to the world generally and to Central America in particular.

But what is the shape of "freedom" within our client regimes in that region? In El Salvador it has taken the form of death, rape, and mutilation of thousands of civilians by death squads and government troops. The types of torture reported to Amnesty International include beatings, sexual abuse, use of chemicals, mock executions, and the burning of flesh with sulphuric acid. According to Amnesty International, "the units responsible for these abuses have included El Salvador's regular armed forces, naval as well as land forces, and special security forces such as the National Guard, the National Police and the Treasury Police."[7]

In Guatemala, until recently, whoever happened to be in power met dissent with torture. During the Lucas Garcia period (1978–1982), those who "disappeared" were discovered, says Amnesty International, with "cigarette burns, castration, traces of insecticide in the hair indicating the use of a 'capucha', a hood impregnated with noxious chemicals, allegedly used to the point of suffocation, multiple slashing often inflicted with Machetes, sometimes severing entire limbs."[8] After a new government took power, nothing changed. In July 1982, Amnesty International issued a special briefing paper, *Massive Extrajudicial Executions in Rural Areas Under the Government of General Afrain Rios Montt*, which concluded that Guatemalan government troops continued "the widespread use of torture and the killing of large numbers of rural noncombatant civilians including young children."[9] On January 14, 1986, Vinicio Cerezo took office as Guatemala's first civilian president in sixteen years. However, it is likely that savage human rights violations will soon return.

Honduras, the centerpiece of U.S. military operations in Central America, has been instrumental in supporting indiscriminate attacks, including the use of torture and mutilation, on fleeing Salvadoran refugees, mostly women and children. According to Amnesty International, "on a number of occasions torture has led to deaths of prisoners in custody, as well as of non-combatant civilians killed by soldiers carrying out counter-insurgency operations in areas near the Salvadoran border."[10]

These are the "democracies," the outposts of "freedom" with which we identify. What is the nature of our military assistance and involvement?

El Salvador is by far the largest recipient of U.S. weapons and training in Central America. Here we have provided aircraft (including AWACS for reconnaissance missions), pilots, advisors, and AC-47 gunships. We have trained over 6,400 Salvadoran soldiers, sailors, and airmen. In addition, we have military specialists (intelligence collectors) with the Salvadoran Defense Attache's office, a military group that supervises the advisors and the U.S. arms flow, and a substantial number of CIA operatives. The Salvadoran government forces that receive this assistance are responsible for the great majority of civilian deaths and murders.[11]

Guatemala also receives military weapons and training primarily from the United States. American weapons in the Guatemalan arsenal include: ten A-37 counterinsurgency aircraft, ten C-47 transport aircraft, nine UH-1H helicopters, thirty-three trainer aircraft, nine patrol craft, fifty-three armored vehicles, howitzers, mortars, grenade launchers, antiaircraft guns, and so on. From FY 1978 to FY 1983, the U.S. departments of defense and commerce and private American companies sold at least $11.1 million in military equipment to Guatemala. Guatemala has also purchased more than 20 Bell helicopters, many of which have been fitted with machine guns and other weapons.

Honduras is becoming a permanent U.S. military base. On average more than 2,000 American soldiers have been in Honduras since August 1983. U.S. military grants are substantially more than $100 million in recent years. U.S. weapons in the Honduran arsenal include eleven A-37B counterinsurgency aircraft, fifteen UH-1H and UH-1B helicopters, four F-86 fighter aircraft, nineteen T-28 and T-41 trainer/attack aircraft, thirteen C-47 and C-130 transport aircraft, and so on.[12] At U.S. insistence, Honduras now offers refuge to the contras, a concession to superpower blackmail that threatens to produce war with Nicaragua.

Our mistake is always the same. Failing to understand that revolutionary movements in Latin America are caused by long-established patterns of repression, we localize all evil in the Soviet Union. Hence we continue to act against our own interests, sustaining a condition of enmity that obscures all understanding. In the words of Octavio Paz:

> the revolts and agitations that are unsettling our continent, especially Central America, are not the result of a Russo-Cuban conspiracy, nor of the machinations of international communism, as US government spokesmen keep repeating. We all know that these movements have been caused by the social injustices, poverty and lack of public freedoms that are prevalent in many Latin American countries. The Soviets did not invent discontent; they merely use it and try to subvert it to their own ends. We must admit that they almost always succeed. The errant policies of the United States have had something to do with this result.[13]

The United States, founded upon the principles of revolution, has become the archetype of counterrevolution. Guided by short-sighted economic considerations and supremacist politics, it has propped up oligarchies, spawned militarism, and thwarted hesitant national struggles to enter the modern world. According to Octavio Paz:

> This is tragic because American democracy inspired the fathers of our Independence and our great liberals like Sarmiento and Juarez. From the 18th century onward, for us modernization has meant democracy and free institutions: and the archetype of this political and social modernity was United States democracy. History's nemesis: in Latin America the United States has been the protector of tyrants and the ally of democracy's enemies.[14]

U.S Actions against Nicaragua and International Law

What are U.S. obligations in Central America under international law? As an answer to the question, "What is law?" international law now rejects all solutions that substitute force for justice. Rather than accept a distinction between the concept and the ideal of law, international law now recognizes that concept and ideal coincide. In the fashion of all other legal systems, the law of nations is a branch of ethics. As the supremacy of natural law has always been a part of the American political tradition, and the current position of international law is largely an incorporation of this tradition, this conclusion signals a compelling imperative for change in U.S. foreign policy toward Central America.

There are two overarching problems with U.S. actions against Nicaragua under international law: their intrinsically illegal character and persistent U.S. unwillingness to submit to World Court jurisdiction. According to Article 94, paragraph 1, of the UN Charter, which is the major law-making treaty: "Each member of the United Nations undertakes to comply with the decision of the International Court of Justice in any case to which it is a party." Although the United States argued that the ICJ did not have jurisdiction to decide upon the Nicaraguan complaint on its own merits, the court on November 26, 1984, rejected this argument. In response, the United

States, in clear violation of the obligations created at Article 36, paragraph 6, of the Statute of the International Court of Justice, withdrew on January 18, 1985, from any further participation in the merits phase of litigation.

No legally defensible argument exists for a foreign policy that relies preeminently on military force and the threat of armed coercion. According to Article 2 (3) of the UN Charter: "All members shall settle their international disputes by peaceful means in such a manner that international peace and security, and justice, are not endangered." This binding norm notwithstanding, U.S. policy toward Nicaragua has been founded on the use of military pressure to produce a settlement favorable to the United States.

The clear impermissibility of U.S. actions against Nicaragua can be extrapolated from Article 2, paragraph 4, of the charter: "All members shall refrain in their international relations from the threat or use of force against the territorial integrity or political independence of any state, or in any other manner inconsistent with the Purposes of the United Nations." These actions, which were never authorized by the UN Security Council or by an authoritative regional organization, also violate other binding treaty obligations. According to Article 20 of the Organization of American States (OAS) Charter: "The territory of a state is inviolable; it may not be the object, even temporarily, of military occupation or of other measures of force taken by another State, directly or indirectly." Article I of the Rio Treaty establishes that "the High Contracting Parties formally condemn war and undertake in their international relations not to resort to the threat or use of force in any manner inconsistent with the provisions of the Charter of the United Nations or of this Treaty."

Another hemispheric treaty that points unambiguously to U.S. aggression against Nicaragua is the 1928 Convention on the Duties and Rights of States in the Event of Civil Strife. Article I of this treaty, to which both the United States and Nicaragua are parties, establishes that "the contracting States bind themselves to observe the following rules with regard to civil strife in another one of them: *First*: To use all means at their disposal to prevent the inhabitants of their territory, nationals or aliens, from participating in, gathering elements, crossing the boundary or sailing from their territory for the purpose of starting or promoting civil strife."

In addition, the UN General Assembly's 1970 Declaration on Friendly Relations, adopted by consensus and with U.S. approval, offered the following authoritative elucidation of Article 2 (4): "Every State has the duty to refrain from organizing or encouraging the organization of irregular forces or armed bands, including mercenaries, for incursion into the territory of another State."

U.S. Politicization of Claims Brought by Nicaragua

The Reagan administration rejected Nicaraguan claims before the ICJ in part on the ground that the court had become politicized and that issues before it were no longer dealt with on their merits. President Reagan intimated that the ICJ is not a court "in the true sense of the word," that it does not consist of disinterested parties, and that it is primarily antidemocratic, anti-Western, and anti-United States. This argument, which apparently did not obtain when the United States brought a complaint against Iran on November 29, 1979, depends on a highly particularistic definition of "political" and stands in ironic contrast to American responses to the Nicaraguan claim.

From the beginning, the Reagan administration attempted to defend its manifold assaults upon the sovereignty of Nicaragua by discrediting the Sandinista regime. The clear purpose of this strategy was to create the impression that this regime was *intrinsically* criminal (because it was allegedly Marxist and pro-Soviet) and therefore beyond the usual pale of jurisprudential protection. If, after all, a state is simply a shadow of an Evil Empire, what possible justification can there be for granting it the usual rights and privileges of statehood?

In support of its position before the ICJ, the Reagan administration relied upon the following political arguments. First, it argued that Nicaragua's request that the court indicate provisional measures to preserve its rights during the course of judicial proceedings "could irreparably prejudice the interests of a number of states and seriously interfere with negotiations being conducted pursuant to the Contadora process." Second, it argued that other Central American states, especially El Salvador, Honduras, and Costa Rica, had rights and interests that made them "indispensable parties in whose absence this Court cannot properly proceed." Third, it argued that the ICJ should decline Nicaragua's request for provisional measures because "such questions regarding the use of force during hostilities are more properly committed to resolution by the political organs of the United Nations and of the Organization of American States."[15]

None of these arguments has any basis in international law. The ICJ had appropriate jurisdiction over the case brought by Nicaragua, both under the compulsory jurisdiction established at Article 36 of its statute and pursuant to the 1956 U.S.-Nicaragua Treaty of Friendship, Commerce and Navigation. Moreover, the U.S. references to the Contadora process and political settlement were ironic in view of persistent American obstruction of that process and the fact that the "hostilities" described had been initiated and sustained by the United States. The only rationale for the U.S. arguments was to bring a contentious matter away from an authoritative legal process, where U.S. defeat was certain, and into a context dominated by considerations of realpolitik, where victory might be assured through military coercion.

U.S. Inconsistency before the World Court

On November 29, 1979, the United States submitted its case against Iran before the International Court of Justice. In particular, the United States charged that Iran had violated the 1961 Vienna Convention on Diplomatic Relations, the 1963 Vienna Convention on Consular Relations, the 1973 Convention on the Prevention and Punishment of Crimes against Diplomats, the 1955 U.S.-Iran Treaty of Amity, and the Charter of the United Nations.[16] The jurisdiction of the court, said the United States, was established at paragraph 1 of Article 36 of the statute of the court. The United States and Iran, as members of the UN, were parties to the statute and were also parties to three international conventions that independently established the court's jurisdiction over the Teheran embassy affair.

On April 9, 1984, Nicaragua initiated proceedings against the United States in the International Court of Justice. In particular, Nicaragua charged that both it and the United States had accepted the compulsory jurisdiction of the court under the terms of Article 36 (a position upheld by the court) and that the court held an independent basis of jurisdiction under the terms of the 1956 U.S.-Nicaragua Treaty of Friendship, Commerce and Navigation. In establishing the merit basis for its claim, Nicaragua also cited the UN

Charter, the OAS Charter, the 1933 Montivideo Convention on the Rights and Duties of States, the 1928 Havana Convention on the Duties and Rights of States in the Event of Civil Strife, and customary international law.

The claims brought before the court by Nicaragua were founded on the same essential sources of international law brought by the United States in the earlier case against Iran. Thus the Reagan administration charges that the Nicaraguan claims were not well established in law were prima facie unreasonable.

To meet its obligations under international law, the U.S. administration need only begin to adhere to its own national legal principles. The basic norms of the international law of human rights have already been incorporated into the laws of the United States. The Department of State is required to enforce the human rights provisions mandated by section 116(d) and 502^B(b) of the Foreign Assistance Act of 1961 as amended. Although it is true that security assistance may be provided to human rights violators if "extraordinary circumstances exist which necessitate a continuance of security assistance," an overzealous discovery of such circumstances has the effect of subverting both national and international law.

In his speech on humane purposes in foreign policy, delivered at the commencement exercises at the University of Notre Dame in 1977, President Jimmy Carter said: "Being confident of our own future, we are now free of that inordinate fear of communism which once led us to embrace any dictator who joined us in that fear. I am glad that that is being changed." The president, of course, spoke too soon. With the advent of the Reagan administration, the centrality of anticommunism to U.S. foreign policy has been unambiguously reinstated. Once again, East-West competition is identified as the only meaningful criterion of national interest and the clearest axis of global conflict.

The U.S. Sanctuary Movement

One very clear effect of this singular vision is the Reagan administration's policies on refugees from Central America. As we saw in chapter 2, these policies grant refugee status to persons fleeing from Cuba and Nicaragua, because these states are perceived as "totalitarian" and pro-Soviet, but typically deny such status to those fleeing from Guatemala and El Salvador, because these states are perceived as *merely* "authoritarian" (that is, repressive but anti-Soviet). Such denial is explained with the rationalization that refugees from "authoritarian" societies are fleeing "economic" rather than "political" oppression.

According to William L. Wipfler, director of the Human Rights Office, National Council of Churches:

> The behavior of the present [Reagan] administration toward refugees from many corners of the world and especially Central America—detaining them and subjecting them to judicial abuse, denying them refugee status, and finally deporting them to their own countries and possible persecution and death—has been a flagrant contravention of the human rights of refugees assured by international law. The United Nations High Commissioner for Refugees' *Manual for Application of the Convention and Protocol* makes it clear, for example, that refugees who cannot escape with documentation in hand, with proof that they are persecuted, should be given the benefit of the doubt in their interviews. Instead, countless arguments have been advanced by US government spokespersons to justify the denial of a humanitarian response and the acceptance of such individuals as refugees. Conditions in El Salvador and Guatemala are not sufficiently hazardous, they claim, to warrant the granting of asylum or extended voluntary departure status to Salvadorans or Guatemalans. They insist that Salvadorans and Guatemalans are largely here for economic reasons, that granting special status will encourage heavier waves of illegal immigration, and that Central Americans coming to the United States should seek asylum in other countries through which they pass.[17]

U.S. policy on refugees from Central America has not only contravened the international law of human rights; it has also subverted the laws of the United States. Incorporating the UN definition of refugee into the Refugee Act of 1980, these laws compel U.S. government officials to base judgments of asylum on whether there exists a "well-founded fear of persecution." They establish no criteria based upon the presumptions of East-West geopolitics.

With these justifications behind it, a national movement to provide sanctuary for Central American refugees has emerged in the

United States since 1982. As of 1986 well over two hundred churches and synagogues were involved in this movement. Several universities and university towns have declared themselves sanctuaries, and most dramatically, an entire state has been declared a haven for refugees. On September 12, 1986, Governor Anthony Earl signed a proclamation declaring Wisconsin a haven for those fleeing from El Salvador and Guatemala. The two-page proclamation condemns the U.S. Immigration and Naturalization Service (INS) for "discriminatory behavior" in denying many Central American refugees while welcoming those fleeing from left-wing governments. Urging the INS to "act in a manner worthy of the traditions of justice, freedom and opportunity long upheld by this great nation," Governor Earl also commended "the many civic and religious organizations and dedicated volunteers working to extend sanctuary to those in need."

This proclamation is not, of course, a legal challenge to the federal government, but it does represent a uniquely authoritative form of dissent from current U.S. policy. Taken together with the imperatives of the United Nations Convention Relating to the Status of Refugees (1951) and the U.S. Refugee Act of 1980, it bolsters the authority of the Sanctuary movement. Yet the Reagan administration has not hesitated to indict leaders of the movement on federal charges of smuggling undocumented aliens and of conspiracy. These are felony charges under Section 274 of the Immigration and Nationality Act of 1952, carrying penalties of up to five years in prison for each count.

Aiding, harboring, and transporting undocumented aliens is certainly a federal offense, but in view of the Reagan administration's disregard for pertinent national and international law and for First Amendment protection of religious freedom, the true lawbreakers can never be those persons participating in the Sanctuary movement. Rather, they are those persons in the federal government who place geopolitical standards of judgment above the law and who bring charges against sanctuary workers without regard for the higher-law traditions of the United States. Even if it could be determined that the Reagan administration's position on sanctuary is consistent with the expectations of the U.S. Refugee Act of 1980, the actions of sanctuary workers would be compatible with the Nuremberg obligations to resist crimes of state.[18] As such, these actions would be fundamentally more lawful than actions designed to uphold the particular codes of a particular nation.

The Nazis and their collaborators committed actions that were not all illegal under positive municipal law. How then could we have prosecuted them at Nuremberg and at numerous other national tribunals in postwar Europe and in Israel? The answer lies in the ancient principle that no statute may abrogate what is peremptory, what is sacrosanct or (as the Romans said) *jus*. Because certain precepts of the law are universal and perpetual, they can never be broken by the laws of particular states. As we understand this issue in the American constitutional tradition, the validity of civil law always depends on its conformance with natural law. It follows that even if sanctuary participants were in violation of federal immigration law, their actions—because they fullfil the expectations of a higher law—are *authentically* law enforcing.

U.S. Obligations toward Central America

"A nihilist," Camus tells us in *The Rebel*, "is not one who believes in nothing, but one who does not believe in what exists." Disinterested in nuance, in complexities that sully simple explanations, the administration in Washington calls us back to an easier epoch when "we" were good, "they" were bad, and nothing else mattered. Ignoring the summons of understanding, it continues to wallow *outside* the world, dissolving thought in the drive for clarity.

But the world is unclear. Pretending that we can endure only in the shadow of contrived ideologies, our leaders refuse to recognize that Central America exists apart from the superpowers. Overwhelmed by dogma, they prefer the comforts of unreality to the strains of learning history. It is not surprising, then, that they steer us toward the abyss without vertigo. They are nihilists.

Our problems in Central America are the same as our problems elsewhere. They spring from a society that celebrates "going along," one that is founded on the absence of consciousness. Encouraging a perpetual flight from self, this society offers deliverance in exchange for subjection. Yet as deliverance is an illusion, it is a poor offer, one whose ultimate payoff is nightmare.

Justice, says Plato in *Gorgias*, is always irreconcilable with the "will to power." As long as our foreign policy toward Central America is purely instrumental, that region will lie outside the ambit of democracy and dignity. And contrary to the myths of realpolitik, U.S.-supported authoritarianism will undermine our geopolitical interests. We must pursue justice in Central America, but this will first require appropriate transformations of life in our own country.

In Ionesco's play *The Lesson*, an aged teacher gives private instruction to an eager but obtuse female pupil. As the action proceeds, the teacher derives a progressive increase of power from his very role as *giver,* as one who prescribes meanings. However arbitrary or nonsensical his meanings, the words have only the significance he decides to bestow upon them. Any other meanings are "wrong."

A similar relationship exists between Americans and their political leaders. Dominated by theatrical manipulations of language, we remain sealed off from knowledge, cooperating in a process that may destroy us. Like the pupil whose subordination drains her vitality and ends in her rape and murder, we too are all too willing to yield. We have allowed our "teachers" to profane knowledge to a point where resistance seems out of place; indeed, to where dissent from official meanings is subversive.

We accept myth as meaning, the demands of an incessant anti-Sovietism as virtue. This is not the cause of our shallow society, a society that retards personhood and national security, but one of its results. Plato argued that our hopes for purposeful reconstruction of social life turn on an intolerance of myth in politics, but today it is the other way around. Our infatuation with a deformed society makes myth possible.

Myth, in this case, brings death. The danger is exacerbated by the accompanying illusion of our collective immortality. Refusing to believe in the possibility of our extinction as a nation, we recognize no compelling incentives for international coexistence. Even the nearness of a planet-wide nuclear winter does nothing to waken us to truth. "Do not try to explain death to me," says Achilles to Odysseus in Hades. "Do not suggest that America can die," command the people of the United States as they stand face to face with the cessation of all life.

Our incapacity to recognize our collective mortality is little more than an extension of each individual's unwillingness to contemplate personal death. The remedy? It is, in Unamuno's words from *The Tragic Sense of Life*, "to consider our mortal destiny without flinching, to fasten our gaze upon the gaze of the Sphinx, for it is thus that the malevolence of its spell is discharmed." Spinoza taught that freedom comes from a cultivated disregard for death, but such freedom is actually servitude. To consider that we must die—and that the aftermath of death is unknowable—is the starting point of understanding, of what Unamuno calls "the very palpitation of my consciousness."

Having bypassed this starting point, the United States now founds its Central American policy on a mordant bravado. In the relatively near term this policy will certainly fail in its own realpolitik objectives and as an instrument of justice. By heralding its indifference to survival needs, the United States will ensure its own inability to survive.

Our nation coexists with other nations in world politics in a perilously fragile network of relationships. This network can no longer tolerate the stresses and strains of structural inequality. Unless the United States rapidly begins to understand that its own interests are indistinguishable from the interests of the planet as a whole, these interests will not be sustained. Instead, they will crumble along with the rest of a foreign policy establishment that is oblivious to its own impermanence.

The Reagan administration's basic commitment to counterrevolutionary destabilization has generated a dangerous kind of aloneness. Unable to free itself from the fatally limiting parameters of a unidimensional world view, it can only advise that "human rights is not advanced by replacing a bad regime with a worse one, or a corrupt dictator with a zealous Communist politburo." Counseled at its highest levels by Babbitts-turned-statesmen, it continues to oppose human rights violations in the procrustean accents of the cold war. Unable to understand the primacy of gross injustice in explaining revolutionary insurgency, it can only suggest that "a human rights policy means trouble."

On October 19, 1981, President Reagan told 60,000 celebrants of the American victory at Yorktown in 1781 that the battle against the British "was won by and for all who cherish the timeless and universal rights of man." The president's address, representing the last installment of this country's bicentennial activities, went on to affirm the United States as "a beacon of freedom" shining on other nations whose citizens are deprived of human rights. Since that time, however, the administration's policy on human rights has been shaped exclusively by the criterion of anti-Sovietism. There has been no concern for human rights as such.

Even if the Reagan administration continues to turn its back on international law in Central America, the victims of U.S.-backed repression will eventually throw out their rulers. In the fashion of Nicaragua, each successor government will join an expanding legion of states opposed to the United States.[19] A sinister parody of its own best traditions, the United States will forfeit any remaining claims to moral leadership, claims that lie at the heart of our widely alleged differences from the Soviet Union.

To act in its own interests in Central America, the United States must restore respect for its own traditions and for the rules of international law. With such respect, the desolate intuitions of realpolitik could be replaced by the essential requirements of coexistence. Newly informed of the differences between violence and power, this nation could recognize that impermissible intervention in the region is inherently self-defeating.

In *The Trojan Women* Euripides attributes the suffering of one people to the hatred of another. In terms of this country's all-consuming preoccupation with the USSR, Euripides's wisdom suggests prompt disengagement from a perspective that subordinates correct and purposeful behavior to ideological distortions. Instead of a pretext for convulsions, Central America could become the beginning of a lawful and productive orientation to foreign affairs. But before this can happen, Americans will first have to transform themselves.

Notes

1. The U.S. argument is that its support of the contras is collective self-defense under the terms of Article 51 of the UN Charter because of alleged Sandinista intervention in the affairs of El Salvador. See *Nicaragua* v. U. S. . . . , I.C.J., 1984, 29–30; reprinted in *International Legal Materials* 23 (1984): 481. In spite of frequent U.S. allegations that Nicaragua actively supports the cause of Communist insurgency in El Salvador, this argument has never been buttressed by any compelling evidence. The Reagan administration's original "white paper"— *Communist Interference in El Salvador*—issued by the Department of State on February 23, 1981, was widely discredited. See, for example, Jonathan Kwitny, "Apparent Errors Cloud U.S. 'White Paper' on Reds in El Salvador," *Wall Street Journal*, June 8, 1981.

   Of course, even if the Sandinistas were involved in El Salvador, that would not necessarily support the claimed justification of collective self-defense. For this justification to be valid under international law: (1) the United States would have to have responded to a request for assistance extended by El Salvador; (2) the United States would have to have demonstrated that such a response was both necessary to halt the "attack" in question and that it was proportionate to this attack; and (3) the United States would have to have reported its resort to collective self-defense to the Security Council. Significantly, the United States failed to satisfy any of these conditions. Moreover, the Security Council voted against the U.S. claim to lawful self-defense on April 4, 1984, by a vote of 13–1, with one abstention.

2. Continuing U.S. support of the contras is in direct violation of the final judgment entered against the United States by the International Court of Justice (ICJ) on June 27, 1986. U.S. acceptance of compulsory jurisdiction of the ICJ began on August 14, 1946, with a declaration issued by President Harry S. Truman, after two-thirds of the Senate had given their approval. Although this acceptance was subject to the so-called Connally reservation, the issues with Nicaragua are not "essentially within the domestic jurisdiction of the United States of America." Moreover, the U.S. argument that the disagreements with Nicaragua are of a political nature and ought therefore to have been assigned to the Security Council (where, of course, the United States enjoys a veto) seems inconsistent with U.S. views on a prior matter before the ICJ—the case filed by the United States on November 29, 1979, submitting its argument against Iran. There is no valid basis in law for arguing that the case brought by Nicaragua against the United States was political while the case brought by the United States against Iran was not political. For an argument defending U.S. withdrawal from the compulsory jurisdiction of the International Court of Justice in the case brought by Nicaragua, see statement by Senator Orrin G. Hatch (Utah), *Congressional Record-Senate*, December 5, 1985, S16920–S16921.

3. See H. Lauterpacht, *International Law*, vol. 3, *The Law of Peace*, parts 2–6 (Cambridge: Cambridge University Press, 1977), 274.

4. See E. Borchard, *The Diplomatic Protection of Citizens Abroad or The Law of International Claims* (1922), 14.

5. According to the opening paragraph of the *Amnesty International Report: 1986* listing on Nicaragua: "Amnesty International's concerns continued to centre on a pattern of short-term imprisonment of prisoners of conscience, and the incommunicado detention of political prisoners during pretrial interrogation. Restrictions on the right to a fair trial and other poor prison conditions for prisoners of conscience and other political prisoners were continuing concerns." (p. 179) A comparison with the opening paragraph of Amnesty's 1986 assessment of El Salvador suggests a significantly greater degree of respect for human rights in the Sandinista regime. Regarding El Salvador, "Amnesty International continued to be concerned about reports implicating the Salvadorian military and security forces, as well as the paramilitary *Brigadas de Defensa Civil*, Civil Defence Patrols, and the *patrullas cantonales*, canton patrols, in the arbitrary arrest, torture, 'disappearance' and extrajudicial execution of people from a wide cross-section of Salvadorian society. By comparison with previous years, when abuses

such as 'disappearance' and extrajudicial executions had been reported on a massive scale, in 1985 violations appeared to be more selectively directed against people suspected of opposition to the government or of being sympathetic to the opposition." (p. 152)

6. The invasion of Grenada by U.S. military forces took place on October 25, 1983. Led by 1,900 U.S. Marines and Army Airborne Rangers, the invasion force also included 300 troops representing Jamaica, Barbados, Dominica, St. Lucia, Antigua, and St. Vincent. By October 30 the invasion had been completed and the island was "militarily secure."

The stated U.S. government rationale for the invasion was to protect the 1,100 U.S. nationals living on Grenada, including some 650 students at the St. George's University School of Medicine, and to meet an urgent request by six Caribbean states belonging to the Organization of Eastern Caribbean States (a regional body formed by treaty in 1981) that the United States assist in restoring political order on Grenada. In view of the president's explicitly stated concern over the 9,000-foot airport runway then being constructed by Cubans at Point Salines (a facility feared as a potential fueling stop for Soviet planes carrying arms and other military equipment to Nicaragua and as a base for launching "subversive operations" throughout the lower Caribbean basin), we can infer that the invasion was also intended to counter Soviet-Cuban influence in the region. Indeed, there is little question that its actual purpose was preeminently to depose the leftist military junta that had seized power after the coup against Prime Minister Maurice Bishop, and then to install a government more to the liking of the United States.

None of these stated justifications meets the requirements of international law. Although it is conceivable that the lives of U.S. citizens were endangered, the actual military operation took the form of a wholesale assault against the authority structure of another government. To meet the expectations of long-standing customary international law, the intervention should have been severely restricted in application; that is, it ought to have been conducted as a limited-purpose rescue mission.

As for the rationale of collective action, nowhere in the operative collective security provision of the 1981 Organization of Eastern Caribbean States (OECS) Treaty (Article 8) is there an option to invite outside assistance against a member state (the United States is not a party to this treaty). Furthermore, Article 8 deals with "collective defense and the preservation of peace and security against external aggression," yet there was no external aggressor. OECS Article 8 also requires unanimous agreement among member states before action can be taken, and that condition was never fulfilled.

Finally, and this is perhaps the central flaw of the invasion's rationale as well as of U.S. policy toward Nicaragua, no state has the right under international law to intervene militarily in the affairs of another state because it finds another regime ideologically distasteful or potentially harmful. Rather, international law expects that every state be free to choose its own form of political institutions under the principle of self-determination. There is no support under international law for anticipatory self-defense if the danger posed is purely hypothetical.

7. See *Torture in the Eighties* (London: Amnesty International Publications, 1984), 156.
8. Ibid., 158.
9. Ibid., 160.
10. Ibid., 165.
11. See "Inside the Fray: Facts on the US Military in Central America," *Defense Monitor* (Washington, D.C.) 13, no. 3 (1984): 10–11.
12. Ibid., 6.
13. See Octavio Paz, "Latin America and Democracy," in *Democracy and Dictatorship in Latin America* (New York: Foundation for the Independent Study of Social Ideas, 1982), 13.
14. Ibid., 9.
15. See James P. Rowles, "The United States, Nicaragua and the World Court," (Paper prepared for presentation at the annual meeting of the International Studies Association, March 1986), 15.
16. See "US Hostage Case to World Court," Selected Documents No. 14, U.S. Department of State, Bureau of Public Affairs, Washington, D.C., November 29, 1979, 2.
17. See William L. Wipfler, "Refugees and Human Rights," in Gary MacEoin, *Sanctuary: A Resource Guide for Understanding and Participating in the Central American Refugees' Struggle* (San Francisco: Harper and Row, 1985), 115.
18. For more on the Nuremberg obligation to resist crimes of state, see Telford Taylor, *Nuremberg and Vietnam: An American Tragedy* (New York: Bantam Books, 1970); Richard A. Falk, Gabriel Kolko, and Robert Jay Lifton, eds., *Crimes of War: A Legal, Political-Documentary and Psychological Inquiry into the Responsibility of Leaders, Citizens and Soldiers for Criminal Acts in Wars* (New York: Random House, 1971); and Richard A. Falk, "Government Accountability 40 Years After Nuremberg," *Journal of World Peace* 3, no.1. (Spring 1986): 11–15.
19. This pattern is not restricted to Central America. As Bishop Desmond Tutu has said, and as we have already noted, it will soon take place in South Africa: "Freedom is coming. We will be free whatever anybody does or does not do about it. We are concerned only about *how* and *when*. It should be soon, and we want it to be reasonably peaceful. When we are free South Africa will still be of strategic importance and her natural resources will still be of strategic significance and we will remember who helped us to get free. The Reagan administration is certainly not on that list." See Desmond Tutu, *Hope and Suffering* (Grand Rapids, Mich.: Eerdsman Publishing Company, 1983), 117.

4

The United States and
the Middle East

A MERICAN foreign policy is driven in the Middle East by precisely the same motive as it is elsewhere: the control of Soviet power. Although subsidiary motives sometimes come into play (and are often mistaken as primary), the respective rights of Jews and Moslems shift in Washington according to the prevailing winds of geopolitics. Usually our strategic interests are identified most closely with Israel. Sometimes Israel falls temporarily out of favor and we seek new bridges with the "moderate Arabs." Sometimes, as was revealed in November 1986, we even seek "better relations" with Iran (which exploits Israel while it positively alienates Iraq and its Arab allies). Only preoccupation with the Soviet Union persists.

All of this, of course, is quite obvious to everyone in the Middle East. In their understanding of what the United States seeks in the region, Israel and its adversaries have much in common. Each party to the conflict knows that the United States detests a vacuum that might become a tempting target for Soviet opportunity. Thus every request to the United States for high-technology weaponry is always cast in terms of improving U.S. influence in relation to that of the Soviet Union. This was precisely the rationale offered by President Reagan in his television address of November 13, 1986, for his secret arms transfers to Iran (transfers that just happened to coincide with the release of certain American hostages in Lebanon). The arms were intended "to help preserve Iran's independence from Soviet domination."

Just how sensible is U.S. preoccupation with Soviet geopolitical

momentum in the Middle East? In fact, although the Soviet Union
has for the past thirty years poured the vast majority of its Third
World aid into this region, its success has been dismal. According to
the *Defense Monitor*, a publication of the highly regarded Center for
Defense Information:

> *The only nation in the Middle East which unflaggingly supports the Soviet
> Union today is tiny, destitute South Yemen.* The other two nations with
> significant Soviet influence—Libya and Syria—both flaunt their
> independence, though the latter has moved closer to the USSR in
> recent years. For the most part, Libya and Syria are Soviet allies
> only when it pleases them and only on their own terms . . . No
> new nations have moved into the Soviet orbit. Perhaps most im-
> portant, the Soviets have failed to take advantage of the revolution
> in Iran and the Iraq-Iran War. Iran remains hostile to the Soviet
> Union, while Iraq continues to move closer to the West.[1]

To a certain extent, U.S. concerns about Soviet influence in the
Middle East are reasonable. Not every effort to counterbalance Soviet power, at least in the short run, is obsessive or paranoid. But
should maintaining the cold war override the imperative to prevent
nuclear war between Israel and the Arabs, these concerns would be
not only unreasonable but irrational. In the Middle East, where the
risk of nuclear war is rapidly becoming significant, our policy must
be to reduce this risk at all costs. More than anything else, our policy
must be directed toward the control of proliferation and the rejection
of nuclear options. Such a policy is in the best interests of all parties
in the area.

Special attention should be directed toward the ongoing proliferation of ballistic missiles[2] in the Third World. Although several
countries have the ability to produce such systems indigenously,
both the United States and the Soviet Union have provided short-
range ballistic missiles to countries in the Middle East.[3] Spawned by
the presumed requirements of superpower competition, these short-
sighted expressions of realpolitik signal an ever-increasing prospect
of regional nuclear war. Since such a war could even envelop the
superpowers themselves, these expressions also signal an enlarged
risk of omnicide.

Israel's dedicated military program to develop indigenous missiles derives largely from an attempt to upgrade and modify less-capable systems provided by the United States. Egypt, Iraq, Libya, and Syria have received short-range ballistic missiles from the Soviet Union. The following table, adapted from a study by the Congressional Research Service, summarizes the current ballistic missile situation in the Middle East:[4]

Country	Potential Launch Vehicle/Missile	Comment
Israel	Jericho, Jericho II	Indigenous development
Syria	SCUD-B, FROG-7, SS-21	From USSR
Egypt	SCUD-B, FROG-7,	From USSR
Iraq	SCUD-B, FROG-7, SS-21	From USSR
Libya	SCUD-B, FROG-7	From USSR

Proliferation among the adversary nations could be caused by uncertainty. Although nuclear weapons can never offer real safety, each state in the Middle East, gripped by fears over the nuclear intentions of enemy powers, may feel compelled to "go nuclear" itself. The fact that the cumulative effect of such thinking must be radical insecurity for all is of little or no consequence. Since nuclear restraint by contentious states is problematic, the benefits of becoming a nuclear power may appear to exceed the costs. Each state may calculate that the rationality of remaining nonnuclear depends on the expectation of region-wide reciprocity.

Further, prospective nuclear weapons states in the Middle East are likely to overestimate the stability of a regional balance of terror. The nuclear arms race between the superpowers has endured for two generations without catastrophic failure.

It is, of course, too soon to claim success for nuclear deterrence between the United States and the Soviet Union. Although it has "worked" thus far (a characterization that leaves out the overwhelming economic and ethical costs of nuclear terror), there is no reason to assume that it will work indefinitely. Indeed, at one time or another, in one way or another, the manifestly apocalyptic possibilities that now lie latent in Soviet and U.S. nuclear weapons are almost certain to be exploited. Whether by design or by accident, by misinformation or by miscalculation, by lapse from rational decision or by unauthorized decision, the system of "deadly logic" will fail.

Nuclear deterrence is a dynamic process that changes continually with momentous and unforeseen effects. Displaying a complex transfiguration unplanned by generations of strategists, the current superpower arms race bears little resemblance to its original forms. Instead of the relatively stable pattern of "mutual assured destruction" (MAD), nuclear deterrence between the superpowers now rests upon a presumed capacity for "nuclear warfighting."

Still another problem of nuclear deterrence concerns rationality. The durability of any system of nuclear deterrence is based on the notion of rational decision making. Yet leadership in the Middle East may not conform to this assumption. On the contrary, the prospect of irrationality seems especially significant in this area.[5]

Irrationality does not have to be synonymous with the "crazy leader" scenario, in which a nuclear weapons state falls under the leadership of a person or persons suffering from severe emotional stress or major physiological impairment. That state might initiate nuclear first strikes against other nuclear-armed states even though enormously destructive retaliation would be expected. Irrationality can be exhibited by a leader free of madness, stress, or any other mental impairment. As revealed by the actions of President John F. Kennedy during the 1962 Cuban Missile Crisis, irrational behavior can be displayed by perfectly cool, calm, intelligent, and self-preservation-minded leaders. Kennedy, we may recall, imposed his "quarantine" on the assumption that it carried a 50-50 chance of nuclear war.

A final problem of nuclear deterrence lies in the overriding egoism of national leaders, a pattern of hubris that points numbingly toward radioactive silence. By denying their own mortality, their own susceptibility to oblivion, states in the Middle East may more readily turn to nuclear weapons. By insulating themselves from reasonable fears of annihilation, these states may make extinction imminent. To halt proliferation we should encourage leaders in the Middle East to associate nuclear war with the cessation of life. Only by rejecting the lethal delusions of survival in a nuclear crowd is survival possible.

This brings us back to the primary axis of nuclear conflict that exists between the superpowers. Before adversary states in the Middle East can be persuaded to forgo nuclear options, the United States and the Soviet Union will have to implement dramatic controls on their own arms race. We must lead by example, not by fiat or intimidation.

How might such an example happen? The answer has already been repeated many times. It lies in appropriate transformations of self within America. The prospects for avoiding a nuclear war in the Middle East—a war that might ultimately claim this country or even the whole world as a victim—rest in part upon a progressive detachment by individual Americans from culturally induced thoughtlessness.

Hazards of a Nuclearized Middle East

Living in a regional nuclear crowd, the states of the Middle East would be confronted with multiple sources of danger:

> The expanded number of nuclear powers would undermine the idea of a stable balance of terror. There would simply be too many "players," too much ambiguity, for any sense of reliable nuclear deterrence to be meaningful.

> The expanded number of nuclear powers would shatter the relative symmetry of strategic doctrine between nuclear weapons states. Some of the new nuclear powers would shape their strategies along the lines of "assured destruction" capabilities. Others would seek more ambitious objectives, including a "nuclear war-fighting" or "counterforce" capability. As a result, nuclear weapons might lose their image as instruments of war-avoidance, a situation that would surely be accelerated by the first actual use of nuclear weapons by a secondary nuclear power.

> The expanded number of nuclear powers would ultimately create the conditions whereby first-strike attacks could be unleashed with impunity, whatever the intended victim's willingness to retaliate or the security of its retaliatory forces. This is because in a region of many nuclear powers, a nuclear-armed aggressor could launch its weapons against another state without being identified. Unable to know for certain where the attack originated, the victim state might lash out blindly. In the resulting

conflagration, a worldwide nuclear war enveloping even the superpowers might take place.

The expanded number of nuclear powers would create the conditions for a "chain reaction" of nuclear exchanges. Even before it becomes possible to launch a nuclear strike anonymously, a strategic exchange might take place between two or more new nuclear weapons states that are members of opposing alliances. Ultimately, if the parties to such a clash involve clients of either or both superpowers, the ensuing chain reaction might consume the United States and the Soviet Union along with much of the rest of the world.

The expanded number of nuclear powers would create major asymmetries in power between rival states. If one state had nuclear weapons, and its rival were denied them, the new nuclear state might find itself with an overwhelming incentive to strike. The cumulative effect of such inequalities of power created by the uneven spread of nuclear weapons could be an increased chance of nuclear aggression against nonnuclear states.

The expanded number of nuclear powers would create the conditions in which "microproliferation"—the spread of nuclear weapons to insurgent groups—might be accelerated. In addition to nuclear terrorism, a possible outcome of such microproliferation might be an anonymous terrorist detonation that could be mistakenly blamed on another state by the attack victim. In this way microproliferation could actually spark regional or worldwide nuclear war.

How might such far-reaching consequences of microproliferation come about? The most likely way might involve a nuclear assault against one state by terrorists based in another state. For example, consider the following scenario:

Very late in the 1980s, Israel and several of its Arab-state neighbors finally stand ready to conclude a comprehensive peace settlement for the entire region. Only the interests of the Palestinians, as defined by the PLO, still seem to have been left out. On the eve of the proposed signing of the peace agreement, half a dozen crude nuclear explosives in the one-kiloton range detonate in as many Israeli cities. Public grief in Israel over the many thousand dead and maimed is matched only by the outcry for revenge. Responding to public sentiments, Israel initiates strikes against terrorist strongholds in surrounding Arab countries, whereupon the governments of these countries retaliate against Israel. Before long, the entire region is embroiled in nuclear conflict.

In this scenario, nuclear terrorism spawns nuclear war. Of course, such a war could encompass even wider patterns of destruction. How would the United States react to these events? How would the Soviet Union react? Depending on the precise configuration of superpower involvement the possibilities are myriad.

Nuclear terrorism might ignite a nuclear war in other ways. For example, if regional proliferation in the Middle East becomes a fait accompli, insurgent groups might commit acts of nuclear destruction and then create the impression that another state was responsible. Insurgents could thus cause a nuclear "retaliation" against an innocent country. Nuclear war, in this case, would be catalyzed by a small group exploiting the confusion of an international nuclear crowd.

Regional nuclear proliferation also gives rise to the prospect of accidental nuclear war and nuclear weapons accidents. This hazard is not simply a function of number (that is, the more nuclear weapons states, the greater the number of existing risks). It is also a consequence of each state's need to compensate for vulnerable nuclear forces by using imprudent command/control measures. In addition, new nuclear powers are unlikely to invest the time and expense needed to equip the nuclear weapons themselves with interlocking safety mechanisms.

Today U.S. (and presumably Soviet) nuclear forces are safeguarded from accidental firings by a considerable array of features built into both the chains of command and the weapons themselves. These features include the "two-man" concept, in which no one individual has the capability to fire nuclear weapons; a control system in which each individual with a nuclear weapons responsibility has been certified under the Human Reliability Program; the use of secure, split-handled codes; the employment of coded locking devices that prevent firing in the absence of specific signals from higher command; and the use of environmental sensing devices that prevent unwanted detonations through the operation of switches that respond to acceleration, deceleration, altitude, spin, gravity, and thermal forces.

It would be folly to expect all new nuclear powers in the Middle East to undertake similar precautions against inadvertent firings of nuclear weapons. To be effective, safety measures would have to apply to all available nuclear weapons and to all pertinent nuclear weapons operations from stockpile to target, that is, storage, maintenance, handling, transportation, and delivery. Moreover, specific provisions would be needed for all unique nuclear weapons system operations, that is, alerts, operational posturing, maneuvers, exercises, and training.

When one considers both the complexity and cost of such safety systems, and the fact that new nuclear powers will find it necessary to disavow certain safeguards in the interest of preventing preemption, the prospect of accidental nuclear war is undeniably very significant in a proliferated region. This prospect is magnified by the specter of catastrophic accidents that do not give rise to nuclear war but that still produce a nuclear yield. Since even the U.S. record of "broken arrows," or nuclear weapons accidents, has included some very close calls, one can't help but anticipate a new rash of broken arrows among the forces of new nuclear powers. What would happen when their bombers crash, when the nuclear payloads that they carry are accidentally dropped or intentionally jettisoned, or when these nuclear bombs or missiles are burned in a fire on the ground? With the proliferation of nuclear powers in the Middle East, such accidents could be expected to occur at an increased rate.

Fear of such dangers is justified by actual events. As reported in the 1986 *Defense Monitor* on accidental nuclear war, from 1977 through 1984 the U.S. early warning system generated 20,784 false indications of missile attacks on the United States. Significantly, "more than 5% of these were serious enough to require a second look."

Today, as nuclear weapons become more accurate and flight times are increasingly brief, both the United States and the Soviet Union, no longer confident that they can "ride out" an attack and still use their surviving nuclear weapons, are moving toward basing launch decisions on early warning of a perceived attack rather than on confirmation of actual attack. It follows, as the *Defense Monitor* points out, that "because the systems that warn of missile attacks are subject to sensor errors, computer malfunctions and human mistakes, a launch-on-warning posture would dangerously increase the risk of accidental nuclear war."

With regional nuclearization in the Middle East, new nuclear powers would face similar risks. Recognizing the hazards of restricting launch decisions until after an attack, they too would move rapidly to place certain systems on hair trigger. In these circumstances the effective safeguards against accidental launch would almost certainly be substantially inferior to those found on U.S. and Soviet systems.

Consider the complexity of our own Defense Readiness Condition (DEFCON) system and the prospect that it could be replicated by new nuclear powers in the Middle East. The DEFCON system puts U.S. military forces on five levels of alert. Although the precise preparations that take place under each DEFCON are highly classified, we know that the entire system works something like this:

U.S. forces are normally kept on the lowest alert, DEFCON 5, though the Strategic Air Command is normally maintained at DEFCON 4. In times of crisis or conflict, U.S. forces in pertinent regions may also be placed on higher alert. The following terms have been used by the Center for Defense Information to describe each level of alert:

DEFCON 5—Fade Out (normal peacetime condition)

DEFCON 4—Double Take (increased alert)

DEFCON 3—Round House (advanced alert—war possible)

DEFCON 2—Fast Pace (full alert—war imminent)

DEFCON 1—Cocked Pistol (maximum alert—general war)

Despite its own internal complexity, the DEFCON system is only one part of an even larger, more complex system of safeguards and war preparedness. Middle Eastern nuclear powers seeking to parallel such complexity would also need to imitate formal evaluation procedures known in this country as Emergency Action Conferences. When the U.S. early warning system detects an event that could threaten North America, four command posts—the North

American Aerospace Defense Command, the Strategic Air Command, the National Military Command Center (NMCC) at the Pentagon, and the alternate NMCC at Fort Ritchie, Maryland—must "confer" via a Missile Display Conference. If the threat persists, senior Department of Defense officials join a Threat Assessment Conference. Throughout the process, military/political judgments are based on information gathered by space-based infrared satellites, ground-based radars, and secure communication links. For a submarine-launched nuclear attack (SLBM), warning time would be as little as five to ten minutes. For a land-based intercontinental nuclear missile (ICBM) attack, warning time would be only fifteen to twenty minutes. Actual decision time might be as little as three minutes for an SLBM attack and fifteen minutes maximum for an ICBM attack. It is extremely unlikely that nuclear proliferation in the Middle East would be accompanied by even this imperfect set of plans and procedures. Regional nuclear proliferation would also increase the probability of the unauthorized use of nuclear weapons. Again, this is not only because of the expanded number of existing risks, but because the new nuclear powers would almost certainly lack the safeguards now in place in superpower arsenals. In response to the need for a quick-reaction nuclear force that can be fielded as soon as possible, new nuclear powers would inevitably turn to automatic or nearly automatic systems of nuclear retaliation that are not "encumbered" by complex and costly command/control checks.

The new nuclear weapons states would also be likely to increase the number of national decision makers who are properly authorized to use nuclear weapons. As long as their early-warning networks are unreliable and as long as concern exists that field officers might not be able to respond to a first-strike attack if central authorization is required, these secondary nuclear powers may predelegate launch authority to selected commanders. Such launch-on-warning strategies would increase the probability of all forms of both authorized and unauthorized nuclear attacks. This suggests the prospect of *intra*national nuclear weapons seizure through coup d'état, a prospect that has particularly ominous overtones in such coup-vulnerable potential proliferators as Iraq, Iran, and Pakistan.

The probability of unauthorized use of nuclear weapons that accrues from nuclear proliferation can also be expected to increase because of premeditated false warnings. The larger the number of nuclear weapons states, the greater the likelihood that personnel who man early-warning satellite or radar systems will deliberately falsify information about hostile action, especially since the new nuclear powers may enforce less than the highest standards of human and mechanical reliability. The results of such falsification, of course, might well be nuclear first strikes that are disguised as retaliation.

The Effects of Nuclear Attacks

The megatonnage in the world's stockpile of nuclear weapons is now sufficient to kill 58 billion people, or to kill every person now living 12 times.[6] Should even the tiniest fraction of this stockpile be used in the Middle East, many millions could die from the blasts of the explosions, the searing heat, and the radioactive fallout. It is impossible even to estimate the synergistic effects of such a multifaceted calamity.

But we know enough! After a nuclear weapon explodes in the atmosphere, it will produce a flash of intense white light that will cause blindness within a range of several miles. The heat emitted by the "fireball" caused by the explosion will itself cause vast numbers of casualties. Even with weapons of relatively low yield in the 10 to 20 kiloton range (roughly the size of the Hiroshima and Nagasaki bombs), second-degree burns will be suffered several miles from the explosion. Within seconds, light and heat will be followed by blast. According to the report of the Independent Commission on Disarmament and Security Issues, which was chaired by Olof Palme:

> It [blast] arrives like a thunderclap, pursued by hurricane-force winds strong enough to uproot telephone poles and trees, overturn trucks, and sweep human beings along at a tremendous speed. The compression of air pressure brought on by the wind and the blast wave itself will crush buildings, killing nearly everyone inside, and loosen bricks and paving stones which will hurtle in all directions, knocking over everything in their path. Anyone in the open or in ordinary buildings within 1.5 kilometres of the blast will have virtually no chance of surviving. As the fireball rises, it cools and becomes a cloud, hovering high off the ground. Beneath it, a column of dust and smoke is sucked up from below. Looking like an enormous mushroom, six kilometres high and four across, the

cloud is a mass of radioactive atoms, some of which are lethal
enough to kill anyone who had managed to survive the heat and
blast effects.[7]

Avoidance of nuclear war is imperative. Even the most limited
nuclear exchange would signal unprecedented catastrophe. The immediate effects of the explosions—thermal radiation, nuclear radiation, and blast damage—would cause wide swaths of death and dev-
astation.[8] Victims would suffer flash and flame burns. Retinal burns
could occur in the eyes of people several hundred miles from the
explosion. Some would be crushed by collapsing buildings or torn
by flying glass. Others would fall victim to raging firestorms. Fallout
injuries would include whole-body radiation, produced by penetrat-
ing, hard gamma radiation; superficial radiation burns produced by
soft radiations; and injuries produced by deposits of radioactive sub-
stances within the body.

Let us consider only one kind of injury that would occur among
tens of thousands of persons—burn injury. To understand the complex medical technology needed to save a single human life from
serious burns, here is an account by Dr. Howard Hiatt, former dean
of the Harvard School of Public Health, offered to his colleagues in
the *Journal of the American Medical Association*:

> A 20-year old was recently hospitalized in the burn unit of one of
> Boston's teaching hospitals after an automobile accident in which
> the gasoline tank exploded, resulting in extensive third degree
> burns. During his hospitalization, he received 281 units of fresh-
> frozen plasma, 147 units of fresh-frozen RCBs, 37 units of plate-
> lets, and 36 units of albumin. He underwent six operative proce-
> dures, during which wounds involving 85% of his body surface
> were closed with homograft, cadaver allograft, and artificial skin.
> Throughout his hospitalization, he required mechanical ventilation
> and monitoring with central venous lines, arterial lines, and an in-
> termittent pulmonary artery line. Despite these heroic measures,
> which stretched the resources of one of the country's most compre-
> hensive medical institutions, he died on his 33rd hospital day.[9]

In the aftermath of nuclear attacks, medical facilities that still
existed would be stressed beyond endurance. In addition, water sup-

plies would become contaminated by fallout. Housing and shelter would be unavailable for survivors. Transportation and communication would break down to almost prehistorical levels. And food would be scarce for at least several years.

The countries involved in a nuclear war would be modern industrial economies. After a war, their networks of highly interlocking and interdependent exchange systems would be shattered. Virtually everyone would be deprived of a means of livelihood. Emergency fire and police services would be decimated. Systems dependent on electrical power would cease to function. Severe trauma would occasion widespread disorientation and psychological disorders for which there would be no therapeutic services.

In sum, normal society would disappear. The pestilence of unrestrained murder and banditry would augment the pestilence of plague and epidemics. With the passage of time, many of the survivors could expect an increased incidence of degenerative diseases and various kinds of cancer. They might also expect premature death, impairment of vision, and a high probability of sterility. Among the survivors of Hiroshima, for example, an increased incidence of leukemia and cancer of the lung, stomach, breast, ovary, and uterine cervix has been widely documented.

Such a war could also have devastating climatic effects. It is now widely believed that even the explosion of a mere 100 megatons (less than one percent of the world's arsenals) would be enough to generate a prolonged epoch of cold and dark. As we have learned, the threshold for a nuclear winter might be very low.[10]

Halting Nuclear Proliferation in the Middle East

The present nonproliferation regime is based on a series of multilateral agreements, statutes, and safeguards. The principal elements of this series are the Atomic Energy Act of 1954; the Statute of the International Atomic Energy Agency (IAEA), which came into force in 1957; the Nuclear Test Ban Treaty, which came into force on October 10, 1963; the Outer Space Treaty, which came into force on October 10, 1967; the Treaty Prohibiting Nuclear Weapons in Latin America, which came into force on April 22, 1968; the Seabeds Arms Control Treaty, which came into force on May 18, 1972; the

1978 Nuclear Nonproliferation Act; and, most important, the Treaty on the Non-Proliferation of Nuclear Weapons (NPT), which came into force on March 5, 1970.[11]

Since Article VI of the NPT calls for an end to the nuclear arms race between the superpowers,[12] the current U.S.–Soviet negotiations on arms control must also be counted as part of the nonproliferation regime. As we have already seen, before the world's nonnuclear powers can begin to take nonproliferation seriously, the United States and the Soviet Union will have to take prompt steps to limit their own nuclear armaments.

In the view of the nonnuclear weapon states, a "bargain" has been struck between the superpowers and themselves. Unless the Soviet Union and the United States begin to take more ambitious steps toward implementation of Article VI, these states may move in the direction of nuclear capability. The nonnuclear powers consider this bargain the most prudent path to safety.

To control nuclear proliferation, the superpowers must restructure their central strategic relationship. They must return to strategies of "minimum deterrence" and institute a comprehensive nuclear test ban, a joint renunciation of first-use of nuclear weapons, a joint nuclear freeze, and a joint effort toward creating additional nuclear weapons free zones. This, in turn, will require an end to the theology of anti-Sovietism and control of America by the herd.

Additional incentives, however, will also be needed. The IAEA must be granted greater authority to inspect nuclear facilities, search for clandestine stockpiles, and pursue stolen nuclear materials. Ultimately, such authority must be extended to all nuclear facilities of all nonnuclear weapons states. Without such a tightening of IAEA safeguards, a number of nonnuclear weapon states can be expected to calculate that the benefits of nonproliferation are exceeded by the costs.

The strengthening and expanding of IAEA safeguards and functions can be served by an improved international capability for gathering covert intelligence. In the future, many of the intelligence capabilities that now rest entirely with national governments will need to be pooled and coordinated.

A final arena in which the nonproliferation regime can be improved is nuclear export policy. Access to a nuclear weapons capability now depends largely on the policies of a small group of supplier states. In the years ahead, these states—which carry on international commerce in nuclear facilities, nuclear technology, and nuclear materials—will have to improve and coordinate their export policies.

The problem with improving export policies is the double-edged character of nuclear exports. Although they contribute to the spread of nuclear weapons, these exports are an exceptionally lucrative market for the supplier states. Therefore, unless every supplier state can be convinced that its own commitment to restraint in the export of sensitive technologies will be paralleled by every other supplier state, the hazards of a worldwide plutonium economy may be irrepressible.

To avert these hazards, two systems are required: (1) a system for verification of compliance with common nuclear export policies; and (2) a system of sanctions for noncompliance in which the costs of departure from such policies are so great as to outweigh the anticipated benefits of export revenues. Without such systems, the obligations on nuclear exports now imposed by IAEA and the NPT will have no meaningful effect.

Ultimately, the effectiveness of nonproliferation agreements will depend largely on a cooperative effort by the United States and the Soviet Union to control limited aspects of their respective alliance systems. Moreover, it will depend on an extension of such superpower control to all prospective proliferator states that fall under the orbit of U.S. or Soviet influence. While this statement seems to exhibit characteristics of a new elitism, the effect of such control would be to bolster world order rather than primacy. Rather than reassert an earlier form of duopolistic domination, a selective tightening of bipolarity in world power processes could significantly enhance the promise of nonproliferation. This is because a tightening of superpower control over prospective entrants into the nuclear club could make it very difficult for these states to "go nuclear." The "tighter" the dualism of power, the greater the ability of the superpowers to assure broad compliance with nonproliferation goals.

As we have already seen, an important part of the nonproliferation problem is the control of many independent national wills. Nonproliferation efforts in the Middle East will always be problematic to the extent that they rely upon volitional compliance. They may, however, be successful if the superpowers move with determination to assure the compliance of other states with the NPT and its associated norms and restrictions.

Before the superpowers can move in such a productive direction, they will have to become far less fearful of each other. And before this can happen, America will have to end its obsession with curtailing or rolling back an Evil Empire, an end to inconscience tied to antecedent transformations of self.

The Reagan Policy on Nonproliferation

From its beginning the Reagan administration has backed off from the antiproliferation stance of the Ford and Carter administrations. It has not only failed to dissuade certain allies from their shortsighted excursions into nuclear commerce, it has also reversed efforts to defer reprocessing of civilian fuel and the use of plutonium here and abroad. Indeed, within the space of ninety days, the administration approved nuclear sales to India, Argentina, and South Africa—nations that refuse to open all of their nuclear facilities to international inspection, that refuse to ratify the NPT, and that either have or are developing means to set off nuclear explosions.

Curiously, the Reagan policy opposes U.S. law as well as international law. Under the 1978 Nuclear Nonproliferation Act, the United States established sanctions against any state that subsequently supplied reprocessing technology to a nonnuclear weapons state. By acting contrary to the rules of national and international law, the administration makes it next to impossible to sustain a viable nonproliferation regime.

Why does the Reagan policy take such a dangerous and lawless form? The answer appears to lie in the cynical view that proliferation is inevitable. Yet there is certainly no evidence that this is the case. Moreover, as Paul Leventhal, president of the Nuclear Control Institute, points out, "to assume proliferation is inevitable helps to ensure that it will be—a self-fulfilling prophecy of apocalyptic proportions."[13]

The Reagan policy is really a function of its overriding commitment to realpolitik. Forced to compare nonproliferation objectives with presumed considerations of power, the administration consistently favors the latter. Thus when India requested spare parts for its Tarapur nuclear power plant, and when South Africa asked for assistance with its Koeburg nuclear power plant, the president agreed to help. Similarly, he acquiesced when Britain and France requested approval to retransfer 143 tons of U.S.-produced heavy water to Argentina's Atucha II nuclear power plant. On November 18, 1983, Argentina announced that it was capable of enriching uranium, a capability that gives it direct access to atomic bomb material.

To improve its policies to halt proliferation, the United States must first begin to comply with its own nuclear-export and plutonium-use standards. Although this country should continue as a nuclear supplier to reliable national customers, it should refuse to supply states that reject essential safeguards or pursue plutonium economies. As Paul Leventhal observes, "this necessarily involves linking U.S. non-proliferation objectives to a wide range of political, economic and security issues with other nations, and not confining non-proliferation discussions to the narrow area of nuclear commerce, as is now largely the case."[14]

If Regional Nonproliferation Fails

Regrettably, although the advantages of expanded controls over nuclear weapons and nuclear exports in the Middle East are self-evident, they are unlikely to be imposed. Nuclear proliferation in the region may be inevitable. What, then, needs to be done?

First, steps need to be taken to slow down the rate of proliferation. As long as several potential proliferants have not yet attained membership in the nuclear club, efforts must be undertaken to inhibit nuclear spread.

Second, steps must be taken to ensure the stability of nuclear power relationships and to spread information and technology pertaining to nuclear weapons safeguards. An all-out effort must be made to prevent intense crises in the region. Such an effort must be supported by technical assistance to new nuclear weapons forces. Since many, if not all, of the new nuclear weapon states will be especially vulnerable to accidental, unauthorized, and preemptive firings, the United States will have to take seriously the prospect of helping these states to develop safe weapon systems and reliable command, control, and communications procedures.

The need for such assistance will be dictated by a number of factors. For one, new nuclear powers, in response to the need for survivable forces, will almost certainly turn to quick-acting systems of retaliation. For another, new nuclear powers will be unlikely to invest the enormous amounts of money needed to equip the nuclear weapons themselves with trustworthy safety design features. In a proliferated region the United States must share many of its safeguard strategies with the newer members of the nuclear club. At a minimum, such sharing must include information about (1) making accurate identification of an attacker; (2) rendering nuclear forces survivable for a second strike; (3) ensuring human reliability in the command/control setting; and (4) ensuring weapon-system reliability through such means as coded locking devices and environmental sensing techniques.

In addition to offering technical assistance to new nuclear weapons countries, the United States will also have to influence the strategic doctrines of these states. At a minimum, such efforts should underscore the deterrence function of strategic force, emphasizing that nuclear weapons are not actually for waging war. Special emphasis must be placed on the centrality of "minimum deterrence" and on the disavowal of first-strike options and capabilities. Current U.S. nuclear strategy creates some major difficulties in leading by example.

Israel and Regional Nuclear Proliferation

Medieval maps often portrayed Jerusalem at the center of the world. From the perspective of regional proliferation, such a portrayal is valid today. Confronted with difficult choices concerning military preparedness, Israel's decision on the nuclear option will have especially far-reaching implications for peace in the Middle East. Since world order is strongly affected by what happens in this volatile area, this decision may have global consequences.

For more than twenty years, speculation that Israel has a "bomb in the basement" has been widespread.[15] With recent news that Israel received from a U.S. company devices that can be used to trigger nuclear weapons,[16] such speculation appears increasingly correct. Other states in the region may now hasten to acquire the military benefits that allegedly reside in nuclear technology. With the atomic secret torn from nature, these states may see no compelling reason to refrain from full membership in the nuclear club.

What should Israel do now? If it has an undisclosed force of nuclear weapons, or components that could be assembled rapidly into such weapons, should it remain silent? Or would Israel (and perhaps the entire region) be better served by moving beyond the current policy of deliberate ambiguity to an explicit declaration of nuclear capability? If Israel has never actually moved to build a nuclear weapon, should it now do so? And if it does, should the necessary steps be taken under the mantle of obscurity, or should they be accompanied by public disclosure?

These are difficult questions. Because there are many axes of conflict in the Middle East, Israel's enemies may feel substantial incentives to proceed with nuclear weapons technologies irrespective of Israel's strategic posture. The value of nuclear forces has already been openly alleged by several other states in the region. Several years ago Ismail Fahmi, President Sadat's minister of foreign affairs, suggested that nuclear status would not only neutralize the ever-present possibility of Israeli nuclear threats, but it would also neutralize the possibility of threats from other aspiring nuclear states in the area (for example, Libya and Iraq). Moreover, noted Fahmi, such status would lead to a technological, scientific, and strategic revolution in Egypt, making it a leading power in that part of the world.[17]

A special problem area is the Gulf. This is one of the few parts of the developing world where surplus funds exist to support proliferation or to purchase nuclear weapons from a third party. Perhaps just as significantly, the Gulf states are exceptionally vulnerable to a nuclear attack. According to Anthony H. Cordesman: "One well-placed bomb on a capital could destroy the national identity and recovery capability of most of the smaller southern Gulf states, and only five to seven such strikes could probably destroy the national identity of Iraq, Iran or Saudi Arabia. This makes the Gulf states vulnerable to both attack and nuclear blackmail."[18]

One possible Israeli move would be to shift from deliberate ambiguity to disclosure, but to couple this posture with an unprovocative "countervalue" nuclear strategy. Yet there is no assurance that such a strategy would not evolve (as it did between the superpowers) into a "counterforce" targeting doctrine.[19] Moreover, the subtle intellectual distinctions between "countervalue" and "counterforce" may have little meaning in the Middle East, where distances are close and intentions often undecipherable.

Some argue that Israel's security as a nuclear power would be high even if it coexisted with several adversary nuclear powers in the region. It is alleged that there is little reason to strike first in a nuclear crowd. In Shai Feldman's words: "Since nuclear weapons enjoy a high cost-exchange ratio against answering or neutralizing weapons, the incentives for preemption have drastically decreased."[20]

But even if preemption could not prevent a destructive retaliation, it could limit some damage. It might well be rational for nuclear-armed states to preempt against other nuclear states if they believe that the only alternative is to be struck first—an alternative that can never be dismissed in a nuclearized context, especially where counterforce strategies are augmented by defensive measures.[21]

Even if it were the only regional nuclear power, Israel would not necessarily be safe. Its nuclear arsenal might have little or no deterrent effect on "small" assaults against its people or territory. Other states and insurgent groups would be unlikely to believe that Israel would use nuclear force under any but the most nation-threatening conditions.

Israel's nonnuclear enemies might achieve significant counterdeterrent effects by means of other highly destructive weapons technologies (such as chemical, biological, or nerve weapon systems), which are well within the grasp of all states. For example, a nonnuclear adversary of Israel might, after absorbing an Israeli nuclear assault, be able to retaliate against Israeli cities with chemical or biological agents. Knowing this, would Israel plausibly threaten to use its nuclear inventory?

It is conceivable that Israel might accompany nuclear disclosure with a parallel weakening of its conventional forces, signaling a heightened willingness to resort to nuclear weapons. Although such a move would also carry significant economic benefits, it would reduce Israel's options to calamity or capitulation. This would almost certainly be contrary to Israel's security interests.

Israel and all other states in the Middle East must soon begin to recognize their overriding obligation to avoid nuclearization. By substituting the dignity of cooperation for the folly of mortal competition, these actors could begin a general and graduated process of deescalation and conflict reduction. Rejecting the self-defeating lure of relentless hostility, they could acquire real lucidity, a pattern of co-existence replacing delusionary imaginings with pragmatic partnership.

For the United States, measures that inhibit the prospect of nuclear war in the Middle East must become a crucial policy imperative. Such measures must go far beyond technical solutions. Recognizing the corrosive synergy between Middle East nuclearization and endless superpower competition, the United States will have to embrace an altogether new framework for cooperation with the Soviet Union. To bring such a framework into existence, the retrograde triumph of mass man in this country will first have to give way to a more promising storehouse of personal meaning, one founded on rejections of the herd and on affirmations of self.

Notes

1. See "Soviet Geopolitical Momentum: Myth Or Menace?—Trends of Soviet Influence Around the World From 1945 to 1986," *Defense Monitor* (Washington, D.C.) 15, no. 5 (1986): 15.
2. I use the definition of ballistic missile offered by Arthur F. Manfredi, Robert D. Shuey, Richard M. Preece, Robert G. Sutter, and Warren H. Donnelly, *Ballistic Missile Proliferation Potential in the Third World*, Congressional Research Service, Library of Congress, Washington, D.C., April 23, 1986, 1: "The term ballistic missile refers to a missile which is self-propelled and guided, with a range of many kilometers. Ballistic missiles carry their own fuel and oxidizer propellants (as opposed to aircraft and cruise missiles which must stay in the atmosphere and get their oxidizer—oxygen—from it.) Ballistic missiles also do not generally need aerodynamic control surfaces."
3. Ibid.
4. Ibid., 4.
5. Even if we could assume that leadership behavior were always rational, this would say nothing about the accuracy of the information used in rational calculations. Rationality refers only to the *intention* of maximizing specified values or preferences. It does not tell us anything about whether the information used is correct. Hence, rational actors may make errors in calculation that lead to nuclear war. Daniel Frei speaks of these errors in terms of "unintentional nuclear war." According to Frei: "What is being envisaged here is not accidental nuclear war, but rather nuclear war based on false assumptions, i.e., on misjudgment or miscalculation by the persons legitimately authorized to decide on the use of nuclear weapons. Substandard performance by decision-makers in crisis situations is particularly common." (See Daniel Frei, *Risks of Unintentional*

Nuclear War, (Palais Des Nations, Geneva: United Nations Institute for Disarmament Research, 1982), ix.

6. See Ruth Leger Sivard, *World Military and Social Expenditures 1985* (Washington, D.C.: World Priorities Inc., 1985), 5.

7. See *Common Security: A Blueprint for Survival,* Report of the Independent Commission on Disarmament and Security Issues (New York: Simon and Schuster, 1982), 50–51.

8. The indiscriminateness and extent of nuclear explosions also violate the standards of international law. According to these standards, any resort to nuclear weapons would be contrary to the principles of *jus in bello* (justice in war). Although no specific treaty exists that outlaws nuclear weapons per se, any use of these weapons would be inherently indiscriminate and disproportionate— characteristics that violate the codified and customary laws of war. Further support for the argument that any use of nuclear weapons would violate international law can be found in book 3, chapter 11 of Hugo Grotius's *The Law of War and Peace.* Here, Grotius speaks of the need to allow innocents an opportunity to escape from carnage, an imperative that is itself drawn from Old Testament accounts of ancient Israel. According to Grotius: "The Jewish interpreters note that it was a custom among their ancestors that, when they were besieging a city, they would not completely encircle it, but would leave a sector open for those who wished to escape, in order that the issue might be determined with less bloodshed." A similar argument was made by Polybius (*Punic Wars*), in his account of Scipio Aemilianus's proclamation upon the destruction of Carthage: "Let those who wish, flee"; and by the judgment of Tacitus, "To butcher those who have surrendered is savage."

9. Taken from a 1986 printed statement of Physicians for Social Responsibility, Washington, D.C.

10. For additional information on the concept of nuclear winter see: Richard P. Turco, Owen B. Toon, Thomas P. Ackerman, James B. Pollack, and Carl Sagan, "The Climatic Effects of Nuclear War," *Scientific American* 251, no. 2 (August 1984): 33–43; Paul R. Ehrlich et al., "Long-Term Biological Consequences of Nuclear War," *Science* 222, no. 4630 (December 23, 1983): 1293–1300; R. P. Turco et al., "Nuclear Winter: Global Consequences of Multiple Nuclear Explosions," *Science* 222, no. 4630 (December 23, 1983): 1283–1292; Carl Sagan, "Nuclear War and Climatic Catastrophe: Some Policy Implications," *Foreign Affairs* 62, no. 2 (Winter 1983/1984): 257–292; Curt Covey et al., "Global Atmospheric Effects of Massive Smoke Injections from a Nuclear War: Results from General Circulations Model Simulations," *Nature* 308, no. 5954 (March 1, 1984): 21–25; and Carl Sagan, "The Nuclear Winter" (Boston: Council for a Livable World Education Fund, 1983). See also *The Effects on the Atmosphere of a Major Nuclear Exchange,* (Washington, D.C.: National Research Council, National Academy of Sciences, 1984). Commissioned by the Department of Defense, this report supports the main lines of argument and the principal findings of the 1983 nuclear winter research team headed by Carl Sagan. The NAS research panel, chaired by Dr. George F. Carrier of Harvard University,

stressed that its findings implied no threshold. A smaller war would produce smaller effects, but the study did not disclose exactly how small a nuclear exchange would have to be to avoid a nuclear winter.

11. The third review conference for the Treaty on the Nonproliferation of Nuclear Weapons (NPT) was held in September 1985. A fifth review conference will be held in 1995 to decide whether the treaty shall continue in force indefinitely. For information on the history and background of the NPT, and on the 1985 review conference, see Robert L. Beckman and Warren H. Donnelly, "The Treaty on the Non-Proliferation of Nuclear Weapons: The 1985 Review Conference and Matters of Congressional Interest," Report No. 85–80 S, Congressional Research Service, Library of Congress, Washington, D.C., April 22, 1985. For additional information on the background of the current nonproliferation regime, see Warren H. Donnelly, "The International Non-Proliferation Regime: A Brief Description of its Precursors, Present Form, and United States Support for It," Report No. 83–127 S, Congressional Research Service, Library of Congress, Washington, D.C., June 1983.

12. According to Article VI of the Treaty on the Nonproliferation of Nuclear Weapons: "Each of the Parties to the Treaty undertakes to pursue negotiations in good faith on effective measures relating to cessation of the nuclear arms at an early date and to nuclear disarmament, and on a treaty on general and complete disarmament under strict and effective international control."

13. See Paul Leventhal, "Getting Serious about Proliferation," *Bulletin of the Atomic Scientists*, March 1984, 8.

14. Ibid., 9.

15. For a detailed discussion of these issues, see Louis René Beres, ed., *Security or Armageddon: Israel's Nuclear Strategy* (Lexington, Mass.: Lexington Books, 1986).

16. These devices, described as krytrons or pentodes, are a type of cathode tube with primarily military applications. According to Israeli officials, they were not used for any nuclear applications. See Thomas L. Friedman, "Israel Offers to Return Some of the Trigger Devices Usable in Making Nuclear Arms," *New York Times*, May 17, 1985, 6.

17. See Uri Bar-Joseph, "The Hidden Debate: The Formation of Nuclear Doctrines in the Middle East," *Journal of Strategic Studies* 5, no. 2 (June 1982): 208.

18. See A. H. Cordesman, *The Gulf and the Search for Strategic Stability: Saudi Arabia, the Military Balance in the Gulf, and Trends in the Arab-Israeli Military Balance* (Boulder, Colo.: Westview Press, 1984), 760.

19. Even if its strategy remained "countervalue," Israel's perceived willingness to use nuclear weapons would be problematic, since civilian populations would be intentionally targeted (unlike a "counterforce" strategy, where civilian injuries and fatalities are "collateral damage").

20. See Shai Feldman, *Israeli Nuclear Deterrence: A Strategy for the 1980s* (New York: Columbia University Press, 1982), 46.

21. An important variable in these sorts of calculations is the precise nature of deployed nuclear weapons. It is one thing to be capable of manufacturing an atomic bomb; it is quite another to be capable of manufacturing a warhead for

nuclear missiles. With a nuclear missile capability, a state's willingness to preempt against other nuclear weapons states may well be enlarged, especially where the intended victim state(s) must rely on more rudimentary delivery vehicles. For an important and useful assessment of the capacity of certain countries to manufacture nuclear warheads suitable for delivery by missiles, see Warren H. Donnelly, *A Brief Analysis of the Ability of Eight Nations To Make Warheads for Nuclear Missiles*, Congressional Research Service, Library of Congress, Washington, D.C., April 23, 1986.

5

The United States and Terrorism

As a problem of U.S. foreign policy, terrorism is often the result of the priority we assign to anti-Sovietism. Committed above all else to "winning" the cold war, we tolerate or support regime terror in authoritarian nations. Since regime terror breeds insurgent terror, we ensure our continued victimization.

We also breed terrorism by expanding the nuclear arms race among our allies. Consider the deployment of American Euromissiles. Not only does this deployment enlarge the probability of nuclear war, it creates the conditions for anti-American terrorism. In response to what they view as American plans for "sanctuary nuclear war," in which Soviet nuclear reprisals would be confined to European targets, millions of Europeans oppose the stationing of cruise and Pershing II missiles on their territories. During the next several years small groups drawn from these millions will choose violence as their preferred strategy of response—violence that could include repeated assaults on U.S. and NATO installations or on targets within the United States itself.

Camus speaks of metaphysical revolt, the revolt of each person against conditions of life. For an effective U.S. response to terrorism, such revolt must be made manifest in America before we can claim safety from various expressions of insurgency. Returning to their own inwardness, Americans must learn to reject the desolate intuitions of geopolitics and progress to new definitions of interpersonal and international collaboration. Then we can begin to disengage from an endless cycle of foreign policy failures—failures that give rise to terrorism against the United States.

Of course, as we will see, even a new lucidity in U.S. foreign policy would not mean liberation from the threat of terrorism. So long as a theoretical global equality conceals great factual inequalities, the spirit of rebellion—lawful and lawless; discriminate and indiscriminate; purposeful and irrational—will persist. To confront this spirit and to transform it from a corrosive to a harmonizing force will not always be possible. But if we are to do the best we can, we will first have to free ourselves from the expectations of theological politics and from the underlying idea that we exist only because of our membership in the anti-Soviet herd.

Our domination by anti-Sovietism has compelled us to support terrorism against "totalitarian" regimes. Our assistance to the contras in Central America and to Unita in Angola has made the United States an international outlaw. Not surprisingly, therefore, we elicit little sympathy from the rest of the world when we become victims of terrorism ourselves in other places.

When the United States supports terrorism against pro-Soviet regimes, it increases the likelihood that these regimes will themselves respond with terrorism against the United States. Indeed, it is even plausible that U.S.-supported terrorists that are defeated (for example, the contras) will become anti-American terrorists. Embittered by what they may perceive as inadequate support from the North, they may discharge their last spasms of violence against their former patrons.

When the United States supports terrorism against pro-Soviet regimes, it must expect the Soviet Union will respond in kind. Although some allege that the USSR is a principal source of anti-American terrorism, little hard evidence corroborates these claims. Should we continue surrogate warfare against the Soviet Union, however, such allegations will become a self-fulfilling prophecy.

If the United States were to disengage from its all-consuming rivalry with another superpower, it would allow the Soviet Union to forgo support of anti-American terrorism. Moreover, it would create conditions in which we might cooperate to curb terrorism generally. At a moment in history when the Soviets seek far-reaching measures toward nuclear arms control and disarmament, cooperation to end the arms race would establish the essential foundation for mutual terrorism control. In exchange for certain patterns of denuclearization, the Soviets might agree to diminished support for states that sustain anti-American terrorism (for example, Syria and Libya).

We must not abandon our interests, nor should we expect the Soviet Union to abandon its interests. Rather, we must understand that basing every element of our foreign policy on its probable effect on the USSR is contrary to our needs.

Once we understand that U.S.-Soviet cooperation is in the security interests of both countries, and that the Soviets can agree with this, we can move toward a genuinely self-serving foreign policy. Founded on an end to the naive cynicism of an endless cold war, this policy would acknowledge the importance of human rights *everywhere* and would strive for *real* arms control. Only then would we find safety from the perils of terrorism.

Contrary to our usual perceptions, the Soviets have as much to gain from superpower cooperation against terrorism as does the United States. They too have vital interests that can be undermined by terrorism. The United States supports a number of insurgent organizations that attack pro-Soviet regimes. A major problem in creating superpower cooperation, however, lies in two fundamentally different conceptions of terrorism.

From the Soviet perspective, the United States uses the term *terrorism* to discredit legitimate movements for self-determination. As stated in a recent Soviet publication by I. Blischenko and N. Zhdanov: "Representatives of imperialist States attempt to exploit the discussion of international terrorism in the UN in order to extend this concept to the national liberation struggle and to various forms of the class struggle of the working people for their rights."[1] In their view, insurgent force against what the United States freely calls authoritarian regimes (for example, El Salvador, Chile, and South Africa) is not terrorism (as the United States maintains) but national liberation. Moreover, in their view U.S. assistance to insurgent forces seeking to topple pro-Soviet regimes (for example, Nicaragua and Angola) is not freedom fighting (as the United States maintains) but state-supported terrorism.

From the U.S. perspective, the Soviet Union uses the term *terrorist* to discredit authentic movements for freedom and democracy. In the official U.S. view, the insurgent use of force against totalitarian regimes represents genuine support for movements of national liberation and self-determination. Moreover, in our view Soviet assistance to insurgent forces seeking to topple pro-American regimes only spreads chaos and subversion. Hence such assistance is alleged to flow not from a Soviet commitment to national liberation or self-determination but from an ingrained habit of nurturing terrorism.

Each superpower seeks to enlarge its power and influence in world affairs.[2] Yet in the absence of expanded cooperation both the United States and the USSR will become increasingly unable to meet the domestic requirements of social and economic well-being. Both will become increasingly vulnerable to terrorism.

How can cooperation get underway? For the United States, the answer lies in: (1) an incremental disengagement from support of manifestly authoritarian regimes and a corresponding acknowledgment that insurgencies combatting such regimes may have just cause and need not necessarily be Soviet surrogates; (2) a renunciation of the right to install future authoritarian regimes anywhere in the world and a corresponding acknowledgment that such regimes would not necessarily serve U.S. interests against the Soviet Union; (3) an end to our lawless support of insurgencies operating against Marxist regimes (the Reagan Doctrine) and a corresponding acknowledgment that such regimes are not necessarily enemies of the United States; (4) a rejection of any insurgency that is carried out against noncombatant populations; and (5) a substantially increased willingness to accept meaningful arms control and a corresponding acknowledgment that such willingness is not a concession of weakness but an expression of real strength.

For its part, the Soviet Union must offer: (1) concrete expression of its public and doctrinal disdain of terrorism[3] by opposing (together with its client states of Bulgaria, East Germany, and North Korea) "adventurist" anti-American/anti-Israel groups in Europe and the Middle East and by acknowledging that such groups are not authentic movements for national liberation; (2) a rejection of any insurgency that is carried out against noncombatant populations; (3) an end to support of states in the Middle East that harbor and sustain anti-American/anti-Israel terrorists (for example, Libya and Syria) and a corresponding acknowledgment that these states do nothing to advance the interests of self-determination; (4) an end to shipments of arms to Cuba and Nicaragua (a quid pro quo for U.S. renunciation of lawless insurgencies against those countries); (5) an end to its lawless occupation of Afghanistan; and (6) a reciprocal interest in genuine and far-reaching patterns of nuclear arms control.

Of course, from the American side, such cooperation will first require the kinds of personal transformation already discussed. It cannot take place amid existing social clutter and the suppression of self. It demands prior recognition of Kierkegaard's refrain, "The crowd is untruth." Or as Ibsen's character Dr. Thomas Stockmann, in *An Enemy of the People*, says in the fourth act:

> The most dangerous enemy of truth and freedom among us—is the compact majority. Yes, the damned, compact, liberal majority. . . . The majority has *might*—unfortunately—but *right* it is not. Right—are I and a few others. The minority is always right. . . . I have a mind to make a revolution against the lie that the majority is in the possession of truth. What kind of truths are those around which the majority usually gathers? They are truths that have become so old that they are on the way toward becoming shaky. But once a truth has become that old, it is also on the way toward becoming a lie. . . . A normally constituted truth lives, let us say, as a rule seventeen or eighteen years; at most twenty, rarely more. But such aged truths are always exceedingly thin. Nevertheless, it is only at that stage that the majority makes their acquaintance. . . . All these majority truths . . . are rather like rancid, spoiled . . . hams. And that is the source of the moral scurvy that rages all around us.

Behavioral Strategies of Terrorism Control

Current U.S. foreign policy is not entirely an expression of "majority truths." Yet even if current policy orientations were dramatically improved, terrorism could remain a significant hazard. Although physical security measures are indispensable in dealing with this hazard, an all-consuming preoccupation with guards, firearms, fences, and space-age protection devices is counterproductive. We require a *behavioral* strategy of counterterrorism, one directed toward changing the decision-making calculations of terrorist groups and their sponsor states. This strategy will be substantially more promising to the extent that U.S.-Soviet rivalry has been tempered or removed.

A behavioral strategy must be based on the risk calculations of terrorists. Until we understand the special terrorist stance on the balance of risks that can be taken in world politics, we will not be able to identify an appropriate system of sanctions. Although terrorists are typically apt to tolerate higher levels of death and injury than states, there *is* a threshold beyond which certain costs usually become intolerable.

To understand this threshold, we must first recognize that there is no such thing as "the terrorist mind." Rather, there are a great many terrorist minds, an almost unbelievable potpourri of ideas, methods, visions, and objectives. To seek a uniformly applicable strategy of counterterrorism would be folly.

On the other hand, in spite of the obvious heterogeneity that characterizes modern terrorism, it would be immensely impractical to formulate myriad strategies tailored to particular groups. What must be established is a manageable number of basic strategies formed according to the principal types of terrorist-group behavior. A "blueprint" of effective counterterrorist action will give policy makers a decision-making taxonomy in which strategies are differentiated according to the particular category of risk calculation involved.

This is not to suggest that each terrorist group comprises individuals who share the same stance on the balance of risks that can be taken in pursuit of goals. Each terrorist group is made up, in varying degrees, of persons with disparate motives. Since it is essential in order to create the necessary decisional taxonomy that each terrorist *group* be categorized according to a particular type of risk calculation, the task is to identify and evaluate the leadership strata of each group to determine its predominant ordering of preferences.

To actually mount an effective counterterrorist strategy, the United States must organize its activities according to the following sequence of responsibilities:

1. Appraise the terrorist group to identify leadership elements.
2. Appraise the leadership elements to identify predominant patterns of risk calculation.
3. Examine an appropriate decision-making taxonomy to identify the optimal type of counterterrorist strategy, that is, the strategy that corresponds with the identified pattern of risk calculation.

In so organizing counterterrorist activities, we can begin to develop a rational policy that distinguishes contingencies of reinforcement according to the particular type of terrorists involved. To deal effectively with terrorism, it is essential to correlate deterrent and remedial measures with the preference orderings and modus operandi of the particular terrorist group(s) in question.

For example, if a group displaying the self-sacrificing value system of certain Shiite factions were to threaten terrorist violence, it would be inappropriate to base deterrence on threats of physical punishment. Here, negative physical sanctions, unless they are devastating enough to ensure destruction of the group itself, are bound to be ineffective. Such sanctions might even have the effect of a stimulus. Deterrence in this case should be based on threats to obstruct preferences that the terrorist group values even more highly than physical safety.

Such threats, therefore, should be directed at convincing terrorists that the resort to violence would imperil their political objectives. To support such threats, steps would probably have to be taken to convince the terrorists that indiscriminate acts of violence are apt to generate broad-based repulsion rather than support.[4] As long as the threatened act of violence stems from propagandistic motives, terrorists who associate such violence with unfavorable publicity may be inclined to less violent strategies.

Deterrence in this case might also be based on the promise of rewards. Such a strategy of "positive sanctions" has been largely left out of current studies of counterterrorism; yet it may prove to be one of the few potentially worthwhile ways of affecting the decisions of terrorist groups with self-sacrificing value systems.[5] Of course, in considering whether this sort of strategy is appropriate in particular situations, America will have to decide whether the expected benefits that accrue from avoiding terrorism are great enough to outweigh the costs associated with the concessions.[6]

The reasonableness of such a strategy is enhanced by its probable long-term systemic effects. Just as violence tends to beget more violence, rewards tend to generate more rewards. By the incremental replacement of negative sanctions with positive ones, a growing number of actors in world politics, terrorists as well as states, are apt to become habituated to the ideology of a reward system and to disengage from the dynamics of a threat or punishment system. The cumulative effect of such habituation might be a more peaceful and harmonious world and national system.[7]

A second type of terrorist group exhibits a preference ordering very much like that of an ordinary criminal band; that is, it acts largely for material gain, however much its actions are rationalized in terms of political objectives.[8] If such a terrorist group were to threaten violence, it would be as inappropriate to base deterrence on threats of political failure or negative public reception as it would be to threaten self-sacrificing ideologues with personal harm. Deterrence in this case should be based largely upon the kinds of threats that are used to counter orthodox criminality.

Threats of physical retaliation will not always be productive in dealing with this type of terrorist group. Even though this type, unlike the self-sacrificing variety considered in the first example, is apt to value personal safety, threats to impair this safety may be misconceived. Indeed, sophisticated conceptual analysis and experimental evidence now seem to indicate that, in certain cases, the threat of physical punishment may actually prove counterproductive.[9]

Contrary to widely held conventional wisdom on the matter, taking a "hard line" against terrorists may only reinforce antagonism and intransigence. Recent experience indicates that physical retaliation against terrorists often causes only a shift in the selection of targets and a more protracted pattern of violence and aggression. The threat of physical punishment against terrorists is apt to generate high levels of anger that effectively raise the threshold of acceptable suffering. Anger can modify usual cost/benefit calculations, overriding the inhibitions ordinarily associated with anticipated punishment.

Negative sanctions are not limited to physical punishment. However, there is considerable evidence that *all kinds* of negative sanctions, economic as well as physical, stiffen rather than diminish terrorist resistance. Whatever the nature of negative sanctions, they appear to generate anger, which causes terrorists to value retaliation (or counter-retaliation) more highly than the objectives that have given rise to terrorist activity in the first place.

A third type of terrorist group exhibits a primary concern for achieving a political objective but lacks a self-sacrificing value system. If this sort of terrorist group were to threaten violence, it would be appropriate to base deterrence on a suitable combination of all of the negative and positive sanctions discussed thus far. Steps should be taken to convince the group that: (1) violence would work against its political objectives; (2) certain concessions would be granted in exchange for restraint from violence;[10] and (3) certain physically punishing or otherwise negative acts of retaliation would be meted out if violence were undertaken.

In deciding on what exactly constitutes a suitable configuration of sanctions, America will have to be especially discriminating in its manner of brandishing threats of physical punishment. Threats of mild punishment may have a greater deterrent effect than threats of severity. Mild threats—when severe threats are expected—may even appear to have positive qualities. Catching the terrorists by surprise, such mild threats are also less likely to elicit the high levels of anger and intractability that tend to override the inhibiting factor of expected punishment. Moreover, the threat of mild punishment is less likely to support the contention of official repression, a contention that is often a vital part of terrorist strategies for success.[11]

As to the promise of rewards as an instrument of deterrence, we may find it worthwhile to consider whether a selected number of concessions would produce a gainful net effect. In other words, recognizing that threats of severe punishment produce rationality-impairing stress, which in turn produces greater resistance rather than compliance, we may discover that the promise of rewards communicates feelings of sympathy and concern, which in turn diminish terrorist resistance. We may thus begin to learn the particular concessions that the terrorists are prepared to make.

Of course, current U.S. policy officially forbids concessions to terrorists. According to the Department of State: "Based upon a careful study of past experience, the US Government has concluded that payment of ransom or other concessions to terrorists in exchange for the release of hostages increases the danger that others will be taken hostage. The policy of the US Government is, therefore, to reject categorically demands for ransom, prisoner exchanges, and deals with terrorists in exchange for hostage release."[12]

Yet we know—especially since the events of November 1986 when the Reagan administration delivered arms to Iran in exchange for U.S. hostages in Lebanon—that broad statements of abstract policy are unimportant in themselves. As long as American decision makers in particular circumstances perceive that the benefits to be obtained from concessions to terrorists outweigh the costs, they will violate their own policies. As long as we are repulsed by the prospect of dealing with terrorists, the most effective strategy of counterterrorism lies in removing (as far as possible) the political grievances that give rise to anti-American violence in the first place.

A fourth and final type of terrorist group is spurred on by the need for spectacular self-assertion. From the standpoint of preventing violence, this type of terrorist presents the greatest problem. Since the preference that would need to be obstructed in this case is neither political success nor personal profit but the violent act itself, and since personal safety is unlikely to figure importantly in the terrorist risk calculation, deterrence of terrorism must be abandoned altogether as a viable strategy. Instead, all preventive measures must concentrate on limiting the influence of such terrorists within their particular groups and maintaining a safe distance between such terrorists and the implements of violence, especially higher-order weapons.

If the apparent danger is great enough, governments may feel compelled to resort to a "no holds barred" counterterrorist campaign. In such cases governments must be aware that the inclination to escalate violence signifies the erosion of power. The imprudent escalation of violence by public authorities can destroy power. Taken to its outermost limits, such escalation can lead to rule by sheer violence and the substitution of "official" terror for insurgent terror.

Terrorism Control at the International Level

Counterterrorist strategies within states require differentiating sanctions according to the particular type of terrorist group involved. Since terrorism might take place across national boundaries, the basic principles of these strategies must also be applied internationally.

Of course, special difficulties are involved in implementing behavioral measures of counterterrorism internationally. Certain states sponsor and host terrorist groups and extend the privileges of sovereignty to insurgents on their land. While international law forbids a state to allow its territory to be used as a base for aggressive operations against another state with which it is not at war, a state that seeks to deal with terrorists hosted in another state is still in a very difficult position.

To cope with these difficulties, like-minded governments must create special patterns of international cooperation. These patterns must be based on the idea that even sovereignty must yield to the requirements of justice. Particular states must agree to give protection and support for responsible acts of counterterrorism.

Such arrangements must entail plans for cooperative intelligence gathering on terrorism activities and for exchange of information; an expanded and refined tapestry of agreements on extradition of terrorists; multilateral forces to infiltrate terrorist organizations and, if necessary, to take action against them; and counterterrorism emergency medical networks. Such arrangements might also entail limited and particular acts of cooperation between states directed toward effective counterterrorism.

To implement such arrangements, the United States must continue to enact appropriate enabling legislation. For example, under current U.S. law, 18 USC 1203 (Act for the Prevention and Punishment of the Crime of Hostage-Taking, enacted October 1984 in implementation of the UN convention on hostage taking), the seizure of an American national as a hostage anywhere in the world is a crime in our domestic legal order. Such seizure, including any hostage taking in which the U.S. government is a target of the hostage taker's demands or in which the hostage taker is a U.S. national, is now subject to investigation by the Federal Bureau of Investigation and prosecution by federal authorities. Private persons who aid and abet the hostage taking, conceal knowledge of it from the authorities, or obstruct its investigation may also be in violation of U.S. law.[13]

International arrangements for counterterrorist cooperation must also include sanctions for states that sponsor or support terrorist groups and activities.[14] Such sanctions may include carrots as well as sticks. Until every state in the world system calculates that support of counterterrorist measures is in its own interests, individual terrorist groups will have reason and opportunity to mount their violent excursions.

Effective cooperation in sanctioning states that support terrorism can never realistically be expected. Different states have varying definitions of terrorism, and the presumed imperatives of realpolitik compel particular states to support certain insurgencies or individual acts of violence. For example, during 1986 France joined in the European Community's sanctions against Syria (because of Syrian support for terrorism in the Middle East) while privately making concessions to Syria to liberate French hostages in Lebanon. Moreover, the French government sponsored at least one terrorist act itself. Late in the night of July 10, 1985, well-trained underwater saboteurs from the *Direction Générale de la Sécurité Extérieure* destroyed the Greenpeace flagship *Rainbow Warrior* at her berth in Auckland Harbour. The explosions killed crewman/photographer Fernando Pereira, a Dutch national, who was trapped in his cabin below decks. The United States during 1986 continued to lament anti-American terrorism in Europe and the Middle East while it simultaneously supported terrorism against Nicaragua and Angola. And while the Reagan administration pleaded with its European allies to sanction Syria (only a few months after U.S. bombing of Libya for alleged support of terrorism), secret American deals were underway with Iran to secure the release of U.S. hostages in Lebanon.

The underlying problem is realpolitik. Until the separate states in world politics have genuinely common goals, cooperation against terrorism will be impossible. Although the creation of such common goals is certainly elusive, it can be done. The first obligation of the United States is to move to end the mutually destructive polarity of Soviet-American relations.

Terrorism Control and International Law

The international legal order has tried to cope with transnational terrorism since 1937, when the League of Nations produced two conventions to deal with the problem. These conventions proscribed acts of terror violence against public officials, criminalized the impairment of property and the infliction of general injuries by citizens of one state against those of another, and sought to create an International Criminal Court with jurisdiction over terrorist crimes. The advent of World War II, however, prevented the ratification of either document.

An international criminal court is unlikely to come into being. But there are other measures under international law that could and should be used as international counterterrorism measures.

First, the principle of *aut dedere aut punire* (extradite or prosecute) must be applied to all acts of terrorism. If states refuse to comply with this requirement (normally because of some combination of political and geopolitical considerations), other states may apprehend the terrorists on behalf of the community of nations. A case in point is the October 1985 hijacking by Palestinian terrorists of the Italian cruise ship *Achille Lauro*. When Egypt, which had been holding the hijackers, decided unilaterally to release them to the custody of the

PLO, the Egyptian airliner carrying the hijackers was intercepted by U.S. Navy warplanes and forced to land in Italy. Although the interception contravened a number of existing civil aviation conventions as well as elements of customary international law, it was in a higher sense a *law-enforcing* action. This is because the prerogatives of sovereignty are not absolute; they cannot be invoked to preempt punishment of a major crime committed against the nationals of another state (a crime, in this case, involving the murder of a disabled American tourist).

To ensure the rule of law in world affairs, states have long agreed to abide by the "extradite or prosecute" formula in matters concerning terrorism. By its failure to abide by this formula, Egypt forfeited its ordinary immunity from interference with its flag-carrying aircraft. The fact that Egypt had intended to surrender the terrorists to the custody of the PLO had no bearing under international law because nonstate organizations, lacking legal personality, have no jurisdiction. In the absence of any authoritative and capable central institutions, the rules of international law could be enforced only by individual states (in this case, very properly, by the United States).

Second, the customary excepting of political offenses as reason for extradition must be abolished for all acts of terrorism. Although such abolition would appear to impair the prospects of even those legitimate rights to self-determination and human rights, persons proclaiming such rights cannot be exempted from the prevailing norms of humanitarian international law. The ideological motives of the accused should not be given too much weight by states acting upon extradition requests. While ideological motive should be considered as a mitigating factor in the imposition of punishment, it must not be regarded as the basis for automatic immunity from extradition.

Of course, law follows politics, and individual states normally base their extradition judgments on narrow political grounds. American strategies of counterterrorism should focus on means to convince other states that their own long-term interests can never be served by proterrorist extradition decisions. To fail to recognize these strategies is to commit the fallacy of "legalism" in the search for counterterrorist procedures.

This does not mean that the search for a fair, precise, and comprehensive set of guidelines concerning jurisdiction and extradition should be abandoned altogether. Quite the contrary! Such guidelines could assist states in harmonizing their own judgments of self-interest with explicit norms of international law.

Of course, before anything else, America must apply appropriate criteria to distinguish between lawful claims for human rights and/or self-determination and unlawful acts of terror. Given the context of a decentralized system of international law, individual states must bear the ultimate responsibility for distinguishing between terrorists and freedom fighters. These distinctions, as we discussed in chapter 2, must take account of particular regimes' respect for the international law of human rights, and of insurgent regard for internationally accepted standards governing the use of force. By itself, suffering cannot justify indiscriminateness and disproportionality by insurgents.

It is also imperative that American definitions of terrorism be understood and applied without regard for anti-Sovietism. Before we can reasonably indict acts of terrorism committed against U.S. interests we will need to renounce the Reagan Doctrine. To do otherwise would expose us to widespread charges of hypocrisy, charges that would mock our claims to righteousness as they weaken our political influence. Left unchanged, our inconsistent policies toward terrorism will generate worldwide indifference to American indignation and far-reaching constraints on American power.

Terrorism is not a problem of East versus West. It is not, as the title of a new book suggests, a question of "how the West can win."[15] Goodness and badness are not properties of geography. Some states in the West, including our own, sustain terrorists in one part of the globe while they oppose terrorists elsewhere. Some states in the West violate the most peremptory rules of human rights in a fashion that compels law-enforcing insurgencies. Some states in the East act in exactly the same fashion.

For us, fighting terrorism can never be a matter of standing up to the East (which is, of course, a caricatural description). It must be a matter of upholding human rights *everywhere* and of seeking peace between all nations. This means more than anything else that we supplant the self-destructive antithesis of East and West with a concern for worldwide cooperation. This, in turn, requires that we escape from the prison-world of contrived ideological oppositions.

The root of our problems is always the same, a consuming preoccupation with the Soviet Union. This preoccupation is a product of American satisfaction with life as a "crowd," a satisfaction that makes authentic creations of self impossible. Before America can deal purposefully with the problem of terrorism, Americans will have to draw meaning from *themselves*—to revolt not against their political order but against the conditions of social and personal life that imprison thought.

"The fundamental codes of a culture," says Michel Foucault in *The Order of Things: An Archaeology of the Human Species*, "establish for every man, from the very first, the empirical orders with which he will be dealing and within which he will be at home." For the moment these "codes"—those governing our language, our techniques, our values, and our hierarchy of practices and rituals—are based upon a lie. Promising honor in exchange for obedience, they warn us that our disfigurement as persons is a small price to pay for national stature and private fortune. But perpetual strife with another nation is a formula only for despair.

In the end, we will either create new codes of American culture or we will disappear. As long as we continue to prostrate ourselves in adoration of false goals for America—goals spawned by a ubiquitous incapacity to locate self-worth apart from membership in the state—terrorism will lurk everywhere. No matter how mystifying our technologies or how high our fences, the terrorist will find penetration possible. To change all this we need only understand that we can never discover constructive rules in preparations for annihilation. Rather, these rules lie in an harmonious new world order of consolidation and cosmopolis, an order drawing its vitality from an abundant source of *individuality*.

Notes

1. See I. Blischenko and N. Zhdanov, *Terrorism and International Law* (Moscow: Progress Publishers, 1984), 10.
2. Significantly, trends indicate a decisive *decline* in Soviet geopolitical momentum. With the exception of Eastern Europe and Mongolia, the USSR has been unable to sustain influence in other states. According to the highly regarded Center for Defense Information, "after World War II the Soviets had significant influence in 9% of the world's nations. They peaked at 15% in the late 1950's, dropping back to 11% today. Of the 164 other countries in the world, the So-

viets have significant influence in 18." See *Defense Monitor* (Washington, D.C.) 15, no. 5 (1986): 1.

3. Although the conditions of cold war compel the Soviets to support various insurgencies (both lawful and lawless), the philosophic foundations of the USSR actually oppose terrorism. In a speech at the Congress of the Social-Democratic Party of Switzerland on November 4, 1916, Lenin stated: "We stand by our old conviction, confirmed by experience over decades, that individual terrorist acts are *inexpedient* methods of political struggle. . . . Only the mass movement can be considered genuine political struggle." Recent Soviet writers reaffirm this view. For example, according to I. Blischenko and N. Zhdanov, the individual acts of terror we witness today are "peculiar to the petty-bourgeois groups and those sections of intellectuals who do not have the support of a particular class to rely on." (See *Terrorism and International Law*, 31). We can also extrapolate from the authors' approving references to Lenin's views on terrorism that the Soviet Union remains opposed, at least for tactical reasons, to the very sorts of terror we routinely ascribe to Soviet support.

Doctrinally, the Soviets today have no faith in terror. From their perspective, such violence reveals a spontaneous character (a very negative feature) and a "divorce from the masses." Indeed, terrorism is seen as foredoomed because it is "subjective," because it represents what Lenin identified as the "result of a lack of faith in insurrection" and "the absence of conditions" for insurrection. Or as Georgi Plekhanov has written: "So-called terrorism is not a proletarian method of struggle. The true terrorist is an individualist by nature [very negative feature] or by 'circumstances beyond his control.'" See "A. I. Herzen and Serfdom," *Selected Philosophical Works*, vol. 5 (Moscow: Progress Publishers, 1981), 467.

Today the Soviet Union officially regards terrorism of the extreme left as an expression of petty-bourgeois ideology and "adventurism." Not surprisingly, therefore, they have chosen to condemn as terrorists the very groups we repeatedly claim act as Soviet surrogates. Recent Soviet publications, for example, include as terrorists the Japanese Red Army, the Italian Red Brigades, Direct Action in France, and the Red Army Faction in Germany. In their view, such forms of terror are counterproductive because they are advanced as an independent type of action divorced from the class political struggle. Accepting the Marxist idea that only mass movement can be considered genuine political struggle, they assert that terrorism does nothing but serve the interests of "reaction."

4. Historically, many violent acts of insurgent groups *have* alienated popular support and been counterproductive to political objectives. As examples, we may point to the *Front de Liberation Québécois* (especially the killing of French-Canadian Cabinet Minister LaPorte), the Malayan rebels of the 1950s, the OAS in Algeria, the Turkish People's Liberation Army, the U.S. Weathermen, and the Netherland's South Moluccan fighters. However, the practice of terror and cruelty can occasionally elicit support and admiration as well as revulsion. In writing about the history of bandits, for example, Eric Hobsbawm has indicated that bandits have often become heroes not in spite of their terrible cruelty

(cruelty beside which some examples of modern terrorism pale) but *because of it*. The hero image stems not from their presumed ability to right wrongs but to avenge. In describing the Colombian *violencia* during the peasant revolution of the years after 1948, Hobsbawm points out that bandits who chopped prisoners into tiny fragments before whole villages and ripped fetuses from pregnant women became instant heroes to the local population. See Eric Hobsbawm, *Bandits* (New York: Dell, 1969). What this suggests, from the point of view of effective counterterrorism, is that to convince terrorist groups that acts of violence are apt to be self-defeating may be impossible in certain contexts. Where resort to terror may actually generate admiration and support, efforts to prevent this terror must center on other bases of deterrence.

5. It is ironic that the mainspring of global security has always been the threat to punish rather than the promise to reward. After all, beginning with studies of child rearing, the literature on behavior modification regularly underscores the idea that positive sanctions are more effective than negative ones. To reduce the probability of terrorism, we must begin to look at some carrots as well as the usual sticks.

6. The idea that governments should engage in substantive bargaining with terrorists that might lead to major concessions is still widely criticized. Today, however, we must face the fact that the execution of certain terrorist threats could have genuinely destructive effects on our system. Recognizing this, the "hard line" unwillingness to bargain and concede can no longer be regarded as a fixed and irrevocable position of responsible governments. Moreover, a willingness to offer certain concessions to terrorist demands need not be construed as a sign of weakness. Not only does it have the effect of buying time while other courses of action are explored, it is a reversible policy that does not necessarily signal continuing capitulation.

7. Some of the problems associated with such a strategy in a world system that is founded on the principles of realpolitik concern the appearance of "bribes." Even if a strategy of positive sanctions is worked out that looks exceptionally promising, the public reaction to it may be unfavorable. Matters of honor and courage, therefore, may work against the operation of positive sanctions in counterterrorist strategies. Another problem with positive sanctions is that some terrorists who display a self-sacrificing value system may thrive on violent action for its own sake. They are unconcerned with the political object or matters of personal gain. Here we are clearly up against a brick wall. And then there is the "blackmail" problem. The habitual use of rewards to discourage terrorist violence is apt to encourage terrorists to extort an ever-expanding package of "gifts" in exchange for "good behavior." Here we must confront the prospect of terrorism as a "protection racket" on a global scale.

8. A variation of this type of terrorist group is one whose overarching motives are genuinely political, but that uses ordinary criminality to secure needed capital. The primary activity of this group often centers on "expropriation," the long-established euphemism for robberies designed to supply terrorists with funds. The history of this tactic dates back to the Russian expropriators of the 1860s and 1870s. Later, Lenin was careful to maintain a firm line between expropri-

ations and ordinary crime, but contemporary expropriators, for example, the Baader-Meinhof group or the SLA, have been far less concerned about such a distinction. From the standpoint of effective counterterrorism, such diminished sensitivity is clearly desirable, since it makes it much easier for the government to equate the terrorist robberies with orthodox criminality.

9. See, for example, Ted Robert Gurr, *Why Men Rebel* (Princeton, N.J.: Princeton University Press, 1970), especially 241–42, 259, 274; Arnold H. Buss, *The Psychology of Aggression* (New York: Wiley, 1961), 58; and Leonard Berkowitz, *Aggression: A Social Psychological Analysis* (New York: McGraw-Hill, 1962), 96.

10. America must avoid the impression that the prospective costs of violence are so great as to warrant any and all concessions. Rather, before any actual incident, governments should create a hierarchy of concessions, ranging from the most easily satisfied financial demands to the most sweeping transformations of government policy and personnel. With such a hierarchy in hand, responsible officials could at least enter into a protracted bargaining situation with prospective terrorists, pursuing a concessionary policy that is both incremental and consistent with predetermined calculations of tolerable losses. Such advance planning might also allow the government to take the offensive position in bargaining.

11. Terrorists have long understood that harsh and repressive countermeasures often work in their own interests. With such an understanding, they have even developed tactics designed to goad governments into overreaction. In Algeria, FLN strategy was designed to provoke the kind of countermeasures that would make compromise impossible. More recently, the IRA has deliberately prodded government repression in an attempt to erode moderates' support of the government and faith in the political system. These points suggest that America give careful scrutiny to the prospective costs of harsh physical counterterrorism strategies. Contrary to the facile conventional wisdom on the subject, fighting fire with fire is not always effective. Sometimes it is better to rely on water.

12. See *Department of State Bulletin* (Washington, D.C.: Government Printing Office) 86, no. 2113 (August 1986): 16.

13. Ibid. The crime of hostage taking to which this enabling legislation refers is defined under international law at the International Convention Against the Taking of Hostages (adopted December 17, 1979) as the seizing or detaining and threatening to kill, to injure, or to continue to detain a person in order to compel a third party to do or abstain from doing any act as an explicit or implicit condition for the release of the seized or detained person.

14. In terms of international law, support for such sanctions can be found as far back as the eighteenth century in Emmerich de Vattel's *The Law of Nations*.

15. See Benjamin Netanyahu, ed., *Terrorism: How the West Can Win* (New York: Farrar Straus Giroux, 1986).

6

The United States and Genocide

E VERYONE who is born holds dual citizenship in the kingdom of the state and in the kingdom of the self. When the claims of state overwhelm those of the self, the possibilities for evil defy all boundaries. Nowhere is this more apparent than in the crime of genocide.

Genocide in all of its manifestations is a crime under international law.[1] Yet there is significant divergence between binding jurisprudence concerning genocide and actual compliance by states.

To remedy this divergence a number of law-enforcement measures have been proposed, ranging from expanded patterns of humanitarian intervention, extradition, and use of domestic courts for adjudication of international proscriptions (indirect enforcement) to the creation of an international criminal court (direct enforcement). In all of these measures, however, effectiveness depends on the presumed imperatives of realpolitik. It follows that before we can expect international law to inhibit the practice of genocide, we must first learn how to align the pertinent norms and actual state practice.

The fact that the Genocide Convention excludes liability when the victims are annihilated solely on political grounds has nothing to do with the problem of limiting by international law acts of mass murder.[2] Today there exists a well-established regime for the protection of all human rights. This regime is comprised of peremptory norms[3] that endow all human beings with a basic measure of dignity and that permit no derogation by states. These internationally protected human rights can be grouped into three broad categories:

1. The right to be free from governmental violations of the integrity of the person—violations such as torture; cruel, inhuman, or degrading treatment or punishment; arbitrary arrest or imprisonment; denial of fair public trial; and invasion of the home.

2. The right to the fulfillment of vital needs such as food, shelter, health care, and education;

3. The right to enjoy civil and political liberties, including freedom of speech, press, religion and assembly; to participate in government; to travel freely within and outside one's own country; and to be free from discrimination based on race or sex.[4]

Taken with other important covenants, treaties, and declarations that together comprise the human rights regime, the Genocide Convention ends the idea that nations have absolute sovereignty when human rights are in grievous jeopardy.[5] The Charter of the United Nations, a multilateral, law-making treaty, stipulates in its Preamble and several articles that human rights are protected by international law. In the Preamble, the peoples of the United Nations reaffirm their faith "in fundamental human rights, in the dignity and worth of the human person, in the equal rights of men and women and of nations large and small" and their determination "to promote social progress and better standards of life in larger freedom."

Humanitarian intervention is one way of enforcing antigenocide norms in international law. Another way involves the use of domestic and international courts. Under Article V of the Genocide Convention, signatory states are required to enact "the necessary legislation to give effect to" the convention. Article VI of the convention further provides that trials for its violation be conducted "by a competent tribunal of the State in the territory of which the act was committed, or by any such international penal tribunal as may have jurisdiction."[6]

Court trials for genocide involve some special problems. First, the International Court of Justice (ICJ) at The Hague has no penal or criminal jurisdiction. It does have jurisdiction over disputes concerning the interpretation and application of a number of specialized human rights conventions. Such jurisdiction is accorded by the Genocide Convention (Article 9); the Supplementary Convention on the Abolition of Slavery, the Slave Trade and Institutions and Practices Similar to Slavery (1956, Article 10); the Convention on the Political Rights of Women (1953, Article 9); the Convention Relating to the Status of Refugees (1951, Article 38); and the Convention on the Reduction of Statelessness (1961, Article 14). In exercising its jurisdiction, however, the ICJ still faces significant difficulties in bringing recalcitrant states into contentious proceedings. As illustrated by the case of *Nicaragua* v. *United States*, there is still no effective way to ensure the attendance of defendant states before the court. Although many states have acceded to the Optional Clause of the Statute of the ICJ (Article 36, Paragraph 2), these accessions are watered down by many attached reservations.

Second, courts of the states where acts in violation of the Genocide Convention have been committed are hardly likely to conduct proceedings against their own national officials (excluding the possibility of courts established following a coup d'etat or revolution). What is needed is an expansion of the practice after World War II by states that had been occupied during the war of seeking extradition of criminals and of trying them in their own national courts.[7]

Which states shall have jurisdiction in these matters? According to Article VI of the Genocide Convention, which holds to a theory of "concurrent jurisdiction," pertinent authority is vested in the state that is the site of the offense or is based on the nationality of the offender. Although the convention does not stipulate universal jurisdiction over genociders, there is now ample reason to argue that *any* state may claim jurisdiction when the crime is genocide. Recognizing that genociders are common enemies of mankind and that no authoritative central institutions exist to apprehend such outlaws or to judge them as a penal tribunal, it is up to individual states to uphold the antigenocide norms of international law.

Consider, for example, the trial of Adolf Eichmann, a Nazi functionary of German or Austrian nationality, under Israel's Nazi Collaborators Punishment Law.[8] Convicted and executed after the judgment was confirmed by the Supreme Court of Israel on appeal in 1962, Eichmann was identified by Israel as a common enemy of mankind whose crimes constituted grave offenses against the law of nations itself (*delicta juris gentium*). Therefore, said the court, "so far from international law negating or limiting the jurisdiction of countries with respect to such crimes, international law is, in the absence of an International Court, in need of the judicial and legislative organs of every country to give effect to its criminal interdictions and to bring the criminals to trial. The jurisdiction to try crimes under international law is *universal*."[9]

Another example supporting the principle of universal jurisdiction in matters concerning genocide involves recent action by the United States. Ruling for the extradition to Israel of accused Nazi war criminal John Demjanjuk, a U.S. Court of Appeals in 1985 recognized the applicability of universal jurisdiction for genocide, even though the crimes charged were committed against persons who were not citizens of Israel and the State of Israel did not exist at the time that the heinous crimes were committed. In the words of the court: "When proceeding on that jurisdictional premise neither the nationality of the accused or the victim(s), nor the location of the crime is significant. The underlying assumption is that the crimes are offenses against the law of the nations or against humanity, and that the prosecuting nation is acting for all nations."[10]

Concerning the broad issue of using domestic courts to uphold international law, the example of the United States may be of particular interest. Since its founding, the United States has reserved the right to enforce international law within its own courts. Article I, Section 8, Clause 10 of the U.S. Constitution confers on Congress the power "to define and punish piracies and felonies committed on the high seas, and offenses against the law of nations." Pursuant to this constitutional prerogative, the first Congress in 1789 passed the Alien Tort Statute. This statute authorizes U.S. federal courts to hear those civil claims by aliens alleging acts committed "in violation of the law of nations or a treaty of the United States" when the alleged wrongdoers can be found in the United States. The particular target of this legislation initially was piracy on the high seas.

Over the years U.S. federal courts have rarely invoked the "law of nations," and then only in such cases where the acts in question had already been proscribed by treaties or conventions. In 1979 a case seeking damages for foreign acts of torture was filed in the federal courts. In a complaint filed jointly with his daughter, Dolly, Dr. Joel Filartiga, a well-known Paraguayan physician and artist and an opponent of President Alfredo Stroessner's repressive regime, alleged that members of that regime's police force had tortured and murdered his son, Joelito. On June 30, 1980, the Court of Appeals for the Second Circuit found that since an international consensus condemning torture has crystallized, torture violates the "law of nations" for purposes of the Alien Tort Statute. U.S. courts, it was held, therefore have jurisdiction under the statute to hear civil suits by the victims of foreign torture, if the alleged international outlaws are found in the United States.[11]

Although this case was a civil suit brought by a dissident against a representative of the Paraguayan regime, the court held, in effect, that torture is a violation of the law of nations and can be redressed in U.S. courts. According to the Second Circuit's ruling, "for purposes of civil liability, the torturer has become—like the pirate and slave trader before him—*hostes humani generis*, an enemy of all mankind."[12] With this view, the stage has been set for further expansion of international law into U.S. municipal jurisprudence.

The obligation of U.S. courts to identify and punish gross violations of international law concerning human rights is roughly analogous to these courts' traditional role in redressing deprivations of civil liberties that occur at home. In the words of Judge Irving R. Kaufman, who wrote the opinion of the court on *Filartiga*:

> In many respects, there is a parallel between *Filartiga* and the Supreme Court decision in *Brown v. Mississippi*, which held that state-court murder convictions based on confessions obtained through torture were unconstitutional. Just as our Federal courts traditionally defer to the judicial findings of state courts, Americans are reluctant to interfere in overseas disputes between two foreign nationals. But where torture is involved, on the state or international level, the Federal courts have no choice. The articulation of settled norms of international law by the Federal courts, much like their adherence to constitutional precepts, is an expression of this nation's commitment to the preservation of fundamental elements of human dignity throughout the world.[13]

It would be enormously useful in the control of genocide if the United States were to expand its commitment to identify and punish such transgressions within its own court structure and if other states were prepared to take parallel judicial measures.

We all know, however, that states are typically animated by forces other than an acutely moral imagination and that the presumed requirements of realpolitik invariably take precedence over those of international law.[14] Before the progressive codification of antigenocide norms can be paralleled by the widespread refinement and expansion of pertinent enforcement measures, individual states must come to believe that international legal steps to prevent and punish genocide are always in their own best interests. Drawing upon the Thomistic idea of law as a positive force for directing humankind to its proper goals (an idea derived from Aristotle's conception of the natural development of the state from social impulses), we need to seek ways of aligning the antigenocide dictates of the law of nations with effective strategies of implementation—strategies based on expanded patterns of humanitarian intervention, transnational judicial settlement, and domestic court involvement.

To accomplish this objective, primary attention must be directed toward harmonizing these strategies with the self-interested behavior of states. Before even a far-reaching human rights regime can make productive claims on the community of states, the members of this community will need to calculate that such compliance is in their respective interests. As David Hume noted, the "common sense of interest. . . . mutually expressed and . . . known to both . . . produces a suitable resolution and behavior."[15] Ultimately, this sort of calculation will depend, in turn, on the creation of a new world order system—a planetary network of obligations stressing cooperative global concerns over adversary relationships.

Before antigenocide ideals can prevail in global society, the major states must learn to choose their policy options from outside the confines of a Darwinian context—a context limited by the parameters of bipolar competition and antagonism.[16] Under the aegis of present perspectives, these states have been willing to abide virtually any evil among their allies in the overriding commitment to geopolitical advantage. Vitalized by their misconceived intuitions of realpolitik, the leaders of the major world powers have abandoned their states to the instant, to induced cathartic crises that carry them away from their ideals and their interests at the same time.[17]

To eliminate these crises will not be easy. Indeed, the only real hope for effective legal remedies concerning genocide lies in the replacement of Darwinism with globalist thinking in world affairs. Such remedies cannot be implemented where states feel themselves imprisoned by a recalcitrant struggle for existence. The presumption of the *bellum omnes contra omnes* (war of all against all) in international society must first be renounced.

The task, then, is to make the separate states conscious of their planetary identity. To succeed in this task will be very difficult. But it need not be as fanciful as realpolitikers would have us believe. Before we assume that genocide is a permanent fixture of international relations, we must consider that politics can change. Since law follows politics, the transformation of lethal forms of competition into new archetypes for global society can give new and effective meaning to antigenocide norms.

The initiative must be taken by the superpowers. Before international law can prevent genocide the United States and the Soviet Union will have to end their all-consuming and protracted enmity. As long as the present condition of bipolar antagonism endures, each superpower will continue to accept the doctrine that might makes right.

Driven by their intense rivalry, these states will overlook the antigenocide obligations of international law. Eager to preserve alignments that allegedly improve national influence, the United States and the Soviet Union, as long as they defer to the primacy of the cold war, will subordinate considerations of human life and individual dignity to the presumed requirements of power. In a manner reminiscent of the Holocaust, which was permitted only because Nazi intent fused with Allied "priorities," today's genocides can take place because *good* states have more pressing concerns.

The problem is always the same. Before the United States can liberate itself from the lethal confines of endless competition with a despised adversary, Americans themselves will have to change. Before the United States can begin to "care" about genocide, Americans will have to reject a society that remains consecrated to thoughtlessness.

Americans suffer not only from unwillingness to think. We also display a far-reaching incapacity to *feel*. Like Roquentin in Sartre's *Nausea* or Meursault in Camus's *The Stranger*, the people of the United States are often creatures of "unfeeling."[18] The passive, affectless antihero of fiction is a mirror image of a real social person, a creature of routine who is not deliberately self-destructive, just prudent; not usually intentionally cruel, just "dissociated."

The problem is aggravated by the flood of information that inundates us with successive recitals of distant catastrophes. Deluged by facts about seemingly incomprehensible levels and forms of cruelty, we have more and more difficulty relating to the tribulations of other human beings anywhere. As Milan Kundera points out in *The Book of Laughter and Forgetting*, "The bloody massacre in Bangladesh quickly covered the memory of the Russian invasion of Czechoslovakia; the assassination of Allende drowned out the groans of Bangladesh; the war in the Sinai desert made people forget Allende; the Cambodian massacre made people forget Sinai; and so on and so forth, until ultimately everyone lets everything be forgotten."

It is easy to forget! The herd has no use for memory. On the contrary, it sees in memory a dreaded adversary, one that threatens to put us in touch with ourselves.

The herd takes pleasure in turning others into corpses. The remedy for this tragedy can never be found entirely within the realms of interstate relations or jurisprudence. It can be found only in diminishing the claims of the herd.

A vitally corrosive synergy exists between "outwardness" and victimization. It is because individual citizens of "good" states identify their own humanity with the herd that they dehumanize the objects of genocide. Deprived of personhood by a society that confers status for capitulation, these citizens find it easy to conceptualize the targets of mass murder as abstractions, as members of some other inferior herd rather than as human beings of flesh and bone. With such a view silence is not difficult to understand.

If, however, our good citizen learned to identify self apart from the herd, he or she would incline toward a different view of genocide. Discarding the notion of self-worth as an adjunct to citizenship, he or she would recognize victims as persons. From such recognition silence could no longer seem tolerable and "bad" states would draw myriad calls of opprobrium.

In February 1776 the American revolutionary Thomas Paine wrote: "The laying a Country desolate with Fire and Sword, declaring War against the natural rights of all Mankind, and extirpating the Defenders thereof from the Face of the Earth, is the Concern of every Man."[19]

Yet we feel little or no responsibility for the victims of genocide in other states. How can we? Because our government informs us that such matters are unrelated to superpower competition (and this government represents the state from which we draw our own sense of self), we are quick to turn to other sources of conversation. It is none of our affair.

If, however, we had meaning not only as citizens, it would be much harder to change the subject. Aware of our worth as individuals, we would feel responsible for annihilations elsewhere. No comfort could be extracted from the assurances bestowed by the official voice of the herd.

A now-famous study conducted by Stanley Milgram at Yale University tested how far people would go in following orders that caused pain and suffering to others. More than two-thirds of the participants followed orders to administer what they believed were severe electric shocks, although the "victims" (who were, unknown to the subjects, actors) cried and begged the subjects to stop. Only a small percentage stopped. Why? According to the studies of Frances G. Grossman, a clinical psychologist:

> When the subjects . . . were asked whom they considered to be responsible for their behavior, the larger group which continued to shock the victims said, "The one who gave the order was responsible." When the smaller group which did not continue to shock the victims was asked who was responsible for their behavior, the reply was, "I am responsible for what I do." It was also found that those who refused to continue to shock the victims did not see their actions as doing something *against* authority. They saw it as an affirmation of some value in themselves.[20]

In the late summer of 1941 Heinrich Himmler, acting as the principal enforcer of "the final solution," addressed an assembly of *Einsatzkommandos* ("the extermination commandos") on the Eastern front. He reassured the men taking part in the liquidations that they bore no personal responsibility for their acts. Rather, he indicated, the responsibility was entirely his and the Führer's. According to the testimony at Nuremberg of Otto Ohlendorf, head of Bureau III of the Reich Main Security Office and commander of an *Einsatzgruppe* in the East: "Himmler was in Nikolaev in the late summer of 1941. He summoned the leaders and men of the *Einsatzkommandos* and repeated to them the order for liquidation and stressed that leaders and men who were concerned in these measures did not carry any personal responsibility for carrying them out. He alone, and the Führer, bore this responsibility."[21]

Why were Himmler's reassurances so compelling? An overriding reason was certainly that the killers of the *Einsatzkommandos* were expressions of the deified state in its "purest" form, a state in which the Hegelian idea (discounting individuality apart from service to the state) of the triumphant herd had reached its apotheosis. Of course, there can be no direct comparison between the active killers of the Third Reich and the passive killers of today's states that permit genocides in other places ("killers" represented by the majority of participants in Milgram's experiment). In both instances, however, the feelings of personal responsibility that might prevent genocide are overwhelmed by a deeply ingrained identification of self with the crowd and by a corresponding incapacity to draw feelings of affect from within.

Let us now consider the wholly different world of Le Chambon, a tiny village in the mountains of southeastern France. From June 1940 through August 1944, the resistance of this village to the barbarous German occupiers was unique. Uncompromising opponents to both the Germans and their puppets, the Vichy regime, the people of this village saved many Jews at great risk to themselves.

How does one understand the goodness of this tiny French Protestant village? According to Philip Hallie, who interviewed both villagers and those who were saved:

> It became more and more clear to me that a certain rule or law or ideal or commandment—call it what you will—was not only implicit in their behavior, but was explicitly invoked by their leaders. The obligations this law laid upon them had nothing to do with sexual morality or professional or business "ethics"; it had to do with matters of life and death, with murder and with the prevention of murder. The leader of this mountain village of about 3000 people was a volcano of a man named André Trocmé, a French Protestant who had one basic moral rule, the commandment written down in *Exodus* 20, verse 13, "You shall not murder." What Trocmé and his villagers wanted to do during those four years of cruelty and indifference was not only to follow this commandment themselves, but also to keep the Germans and their puppets, the Vichy government, from violating that commandment. They were

trying to save refugees from death and they were trying to save would-be victimizers from doing evil.[22]

To a great extent they succeeded, and long after the war Trocmé and two others from the village were awarded the Medal of Righteousness by the State of Israel. The efforts that produced such success were made possible by a communitywide sense of self-affirmation that was based on a total disregard for the wider herd of France. Aware that their place as persons was determined by adherence to certain overriding principles of justice rather than to the secular authorities of the moment, they knew that no one could free them from the responsibility to rescue victims of Nazism in their midst. They were able to value others because they had always been able to value themselves.

The state is an instance of the herd. To prevent genocide, the state must yield its demands to the requirements of personhood. But these demands can never be suppressed through the dead world of ordinary politics. This can be achieved only through the creation and re-creation of self.

Genocide is best described as a *procedure*. Unlike other earlier forms of organized violence against civilians, genocide is both passionless and systematic. Driven by abstract commitments to "purity" rather than spontaneous spasms of hatred and lust, it represents a carefully structured program for myriad executions. Unhindered by sentimentality, it proceeds deliberately, with precision, content in the awareness that in the closing decades of the twentieth century compassion is no longer a "problem."

How could it be otherwise? How could we feel compassion for others when we are unable to feel for ourselves? Indifferent and irresponsible to ourselves, because we seek meaning outside, we find it impossible to feel concern and responsibility for others. To the question, "Am I my brother's keeper?" contemporary Americans reply: "How can I be? I keep not even myself."

The task, for America and the world, is to restore the individual, creating the conditions wherein one may find center in a principle inside oneself. This is not a prescription for selfishness. Quite the contrary! As Nietzsche understood, no productive love for others appears without prior love for oneself. Of course, the absence of self-love does not mean an unwillingness to love others, but it does suggest an effort that is more a vice than virtue, an effort that is extractive rather than authentically giving. As Nietzsche wrote in *Thus Spake Zarathustra*: "The one goeth to his neighbor because he seeketh himself, and the other because he would fain lose himself."

Selfishness, then, is not identical to self-love but its very opposite. Before we can care enough about others to prevent genocide we must learn to love ourselves. And before this can happen we must learn to recognize and discard a counterfeit moral universe that always disguises our real interests as persons, that keeps us under the lethal spell of slogans preaching faith in the shallow goals of success and glamour. Only then will self-interest be made manifest.

Hindrances abound! Numbed by repeated doses of anesthesia administered through technology, bureaucracy, and political language,[23] we find it difficult to discover the way back to ourselves. To a certain extent, as Robert Jay Lifton has written, we are victims of the increasing distance between ourselves and the "anxiety of responsibility," an "animating guilt" that is essential to individual and species survival.[24] For the moment our leaders speak only gibberish, and a nation replies only in kind.

Also failing to take responsibility are our universities. At the moment American universities are committed to a single overriding mission—career training. Tantalized only by vocationalism and the search for funding, they have abandoned the classical imperative to foster independent thought, a forfeiture that signals academic complicity in genocide.

Such complicity has its roots in the Holocaust. Under Nazi patronage German universities gave themselves entirely to the state, granting Ph.D.s for dissertations justifying destruction of the Jews. Indeed, as Alan L. Berger has written: "University academics, first, aided and abetted the Holocaust and, second, ignored its lessons and denied its existence."[25]

What needs to be done? How can American universities disentangle themselves from complicity in the problem of genocide? For a start, these institutions must restore themselves as a community of inquirers, rejecting the calls for "realism" that place both students and professors in the service of death. Revolted by the control of outside forces, the academy must learn to accept independence at any price.

Our task is to migrate from the kingdom of the state to the kingdom of the self. But for this move one must *want* to live in the self. This is the most difficult part of the migration because the kingdom of the state has immense attractions. The risks of living within this kingdom become apparent to most only when the possibilities of migration are gone.

Kierkegaard understood the dilemma. Consider his comment in *The Sickness unto Death*: "Devoid of imagination, as the Philistine always is, he lives in a certain trivial province of experience as to how things go, what is possible, what usually occurs. . . . For philistinism thinks it is in control of possibility . . . it carries possibility around like a prisoner in the cage of the probable, and shows it off."

The "trivial province of experience" must be recognized. Only then can it be indicted and condemned to speedy execution. In America this province is maintained by an endless succession of electronic and print images that distort meaning and suppress self. Taking the lies of such images as truth, we ignore the only real truth—the one imprisoned within us. Because we live in falsehood, we are, as Simone Weil notes in *First and Last Notebooks*, "under the illusion that happiness is what is unconditionally important." What is more, we misunderstand happiness, believing that it can be purchased, together with self-worth, with money.[26]

Socrates and Plato understood that the pursuit of happiness is never the pursuit of pleasure. In fact, they are diametrically opposed. With the pursuit of pleasure, Americans inevitably transform freedom into obedience. Although unhindered by political tyranny, Americans understand that becoming a person must always be treason.

Genocide is made possible by the surrender of self to the state. While the antigenocide claims of international law are rendered impotent by realpolitik, this commitment to so-called power politics is itself an expression of control by the herd. Without such control, individual Americans could discover authentic bases of personal value inside themselves, depriving the state of its capacity to make corpses of others in distant states.

The herd controls in America not through the vulgar fingers of politics but through the more subtle hands of society. Living without any perceptible rewards for inner direction, Americans have discovered the meaning of all their activity in what they seek to exchange for pleasure. Meaning is absorbed into the universal exchange medium, money, and anything that enlarges this medium is good.

But the importance of money lies in more than the purchase of pleasure. It lies in perceptions of what such purchases signify, namely power and affect. Indeed, as the ultimate expression of power is immortality, the most crucial value of money lies in its association with the conquest of death.

The herd thus controls in America by nurturing illusions of eternal life, illusions that can be enjoyed only by all those who have consented to renounce their individuality. Before such patterns of control can be shattered, large numbers of people will need to surmount their inclinations to transcend death through various rituals of self-delusion. Only then will they be prepared to oppose genocide.

From its inception in prehistory money has been understood as an expression of the sacred. Today the state is also such an expression, and it uses money to enlarge its control over the herd. The domain of the sacred has become a monopoly power, and with its extension the individual has all but disappeared.

How does money work its power as a lure of the modern state? Consider the explanation by Ernest Becker:

> Power means power to increase oneself, to change one's natural situation from one of smallness, helplessness, finitude, to one of bigness, control, durability, importance. In its power to manipulate physical and social reality, money in some ways secures one against contingency and accident; it buys bodyguards, bullet-proof glass, and better medical care. Most of all, it can be accumulated and passed on, and so radiates its powers even after one's death, giving one a semblance of immortality. . . . In short, money is the human mode *par excellence* of cooly denying animal boundness, the determinism of nature.[27]

Of course, human beings have found alternate ways of bolstering their hopes for immortality (including the killing of other human beings), and all of these ways are encouraged by the herd. Archaic man seeks to conquer death by living the life of his dead ancestors; modern man seeks the same objective by living the life prescribed by the state. On certain occasions this life requires the killing of persons in one's own state or in other states, a requirement that rewards doubly because the act of killing sustains the illusion of one's own immortality[28] while it fulfills the expectations of the herd. On other occasions it requires nothing more than silence in the face of killings conducted elsewhere, a silence that is requited by public acknowledgment of the good citizen, a virtuous patriot who shall be permitted to enjoy the good life, perhaps even forever.

Notes

1. See Convention on the Prevention and Punishment of the Crime of Genocide, *opened for signature*, December 9, 1948, *entered into force*, January 12, 1951, 78 U.N.T.S. 277. The United States signed and on February 19, 1986, ratified this convention. Although the criminalizing aspect of international law that proscribes genocide may derive from a source other than the Genocide Convention (that is, it may emerge from customary international law and be included in different international conventions), such conduct is clearly a crime. Even where the conduct in question does not affect the interests of more than one state, it becomes an international crime whenever it constitutes an offense against the world community *delicto jus gentium*. See M. C. Bassiouni, *International Law: A Draft International Criminal Code* 19(1980), 40–44. See also Bassiouni, "The Penal Characteristics of Conventional International Criminal Law," *Journal of International Law* 15(1983).

2. According to the language of the Genocide Convention it is unlikely that mass murders such as took place in Indonesia in 1965 (the victims were identified as Communists) or in Cambodia from 1975 to 1979 (meted out to suspect classes by the Khmer Rouge) can be called genocide. Helen Fein calls these "ideological slaughters." *See* Fein, "Scenarios of Genocide: Models of Genocide and Critical Responses," in *Toward the Understanding and Prevention of Genocide*, ed. Israel W. Charny (Boulder, Colo.: Westview Press, 1984). Leo Kuper calls these mass murders "genocidal massacres." See L. Kuper, *Genocide* (New Haven and London: Yale University Press, 1981). Similar massacres were Stalin's liquidation of the Kulaks and Idi Amin's murders in Uganda. In Uganda, although the killings were sometimes ethnically motivated (as in the massacre of Acholi and Lango soldiers in the Ugandan army), there were also instances of political massacres (for example, the annihilation of the supporters of the ousted president and of political opponents in general).

3. An opposing view is offered by Robert A. Friedlander, "The Foundations of International Criminal Law: A Present-Day Inquiry," *Journal of International Law* 15, no. 13, (1983): 21–22. According to Friedlander, "while genocide in theory has come to be labeled an international criminal act, it really is only a principle of public international law and not a mandatory prohibition of positive law or part of the *jus cogens*." (pp. 21–22) Professor Friedlander's argument appears to rest on the prevalence of genocide; that is, on the fact that genocide, rather than effective genocide prevention, is a dominant characteristic of world

politics and world law. "Indeed," says Friedlander, "genocide has been attempted or practiced so often in so many places during the past half-century
that some critics maintain that international barbarism, in point of fact, has
replaced the legal fiction of a world community bound by law." (p. 22) This
position seems to be based upon a particular interpretation of Article 53 of the
Vienna Convention on the Law of Treaties, U.N. Doc. A/CONF. 39-27, at 289
(1969), which deals with "Treaties Conflicting with a Peremptory Norm of
General International Law (*Jus Cogens*)." According to Article 53, "a peremptory
norm of general international law is a norm accepted and recognized by the
international community of States as a whole as a norm from which no derogation is permitted." Presumably Professor Friedlander believes that the antigenocide norm fails to meet this standard because it is so flagrantly violated in actual
state practice. By this reasoning, the definition of "a norm accepted and recognized" is tied to general and effective *compliance* rather than to general acceptance of pertinent treaties and conventions.

4. See *Country Reports on Human Rights Practices*, Report submitted to the Committee on Foreign Relations, U.S. Senate, and Committee on Foreign Affairs,
   U.S. House of Representatives, by the Department of State, 97th Congress,
   1st Session, Washington, D.C., February 2, 1981.

5. The Genocide Convention proscribes conduct that is juristically distinct from
   other forms of prohibited wartime killing, such as acts constituting crimes of
   war and crimes against humanity. Although crimes against humanity are linked
   to wartime actions, the crime of genocide can be committed during war or
   peace.

6. Of the 143 international instruments dealing with international criminal law
   between 1815 and 1982, only two others specifically referred to an international
   criminal court: the 1937 Terrorism Convention (Convention for the Prevention
   and Punishment of Terrorism), which never entered into force because of in-
   sufficient ratification; and the 1973 Apartheid Convention, which states at Article 5 that offenders under the convention may be tried by an "international
   penal tribunal." But as M. Bassiouni correctly points out, political and ideological differences between states make it "unlikely that a tribunal acceptable to all
   can be established or that any direct enforcement scheme will be adopted in the
   forseeable future." See M. C. Bassiouni, "The Proscribing Function of International Law in the Processes of International Protection of Human Rights,"
   Yale Journal of World Public Order, 1982. See also Report of M. C. Bassiouni to
   the Ad Hoc Working Group of Experts for the Commission on Human Rights,
   U.N. Doc. E/CN.4/AC/22 CRP, 19/Rev. 1 (1980).

7. Apart from the prosecution of war criminals, there have been only two trials
   under the Genocide Convention by competent tribunals of the states in which
   the crimes were committed. First, in Equatorial Guinea, the tyrant Macis, who
   had slaughtered his subjects and pillaged his country for a number of years,
   was ultimately overthrown, found guilty of a number of crimes including genocide, and executed. (In a report on the trial, however, the legal officer of the
   International Commission of Jurists concluded that Macis had been wrongfully
   convicted of genocide.) Second, in Kampuchea, when the Khmer Rouge were

overthrown by the Vietnamese, the successor government instituted criminal
proceedings against the former prime minister, Pol Pot, and the deputy prime
minister on charges of genocide, and the accused were found guilty of the crime
in absentia by a people's revolutionary tribunal. Pol Pot, of course, is still free.
For more on these cases, see Leo Kuper, *The Prevention of Genocide* (New Haven
and London: Yale University Press, 1985).

8. See Intl. L. Rep. 5 (Israel, Dist. Ct. Jerusalem 1961). Affirmed Israel Supreme
Court, 1962, 36 Intl. L. Ref. 277.

9. See M. C. Bassiouni, ed., *International Criminal Law: Crimes*, vol. 1 (Dobbs
Ferry, N. Y.: Transnational Publishers, 1986), 284–85. The principle of universality presumes solidarity between states in the fight against crimes. It is
mentioned in the Corpus Juris Civilis; in Grotius's *De jure belli ac pacis* (book 2,
chap. 20); and in Vattel's *Le droit des gens* (book 1, chap. 19). The case for universal jurisdiction (which is strengthened wherever extradition is difficult or
impossible to obtain) is also built into the four Geneva conventions of August
12, 1949, which unambiguously impose upon the High Contracting Parties the
obligation to punish certain grave breaches of their rules, regardless of where
the infraction was committed or the nationality of the authors of the crimes.
See Article 49 of Convention No. 1; Article 50 of Convention No. 2; Article
129 of Convention No. 3; and Article 146 of Convention No. 4. In further
support of universality for certain international crimes, see M. C. Bassiouni,
International Extradition in U.S. Law and Practice, vol. 2, chap. 6 (1983). See also
Restatement of the Foreign Relations Law of the United States, Tentative Draft
No. 5 (1984), secs. 402–404, 443, and 18 U.S.C. sec. III 6 (c).

10. See *Demjanjuk v. Petrovsky*, 776 F. 2d. 582–3 (6th Cir. 1985); cited in Bassiouni,
International Criminal Law, 286. Ironically, of course, recent U.S. alacrity in
extraditing Nazi war criminals to other countries for prosecution belies America's protection of such criminals for geopolitical purposes. Substantial evidence
now indicates that U.S. intelligence officials concealed the Nazi records of
hundreds of former enemy scientists to bring them into this country after World
War II. The documents disclosed reveal that many American authorities knew
that the entering criminals were "ardent Nazis" implicated in atrocities. Specifically, between 1945 and 1955, some 800 former enemy rocket experts and other
specialists were brought into the United States under an American intelligence
program first called Overcast and then Project Paperclip. See Ralph Blumen-
thal, "Nazi Whitewash in 1940's Charged," *New York Times*, March 11, 1985, 1.

11. See the 1980 U.S. federal appellate case of *Filartiga v. Pena-Irala*, 630 F. 2d 876
(2d Cir. 1980).

12. Ibid., 890. Paraguay has been the site of not only individual acts of torture but
also genocide. In 1974 the International League for the Rights of Man together
with the Inter-American Association for Democracy and Freedom charged the
government of Paraguay with complicity in genocide against the Ache (Guay-
aki) Indians, alleging that the Indians had been enslaved, tortured and massa-
cred; that food and medicine had been denied them; and that their children had
been removed and sold. For more on Paraguay and genocide, see Richard
Arens, "The Ache of Paraguay," in *Genocide and Human Rights: A Global Anthol-*

ogy ed. Jack Nusan Porter (Washington, D.C.: University Press of America, 1982), 218–237; and, by the same author, *Genocide in Paraguay* (Philadelphia: Temple University Press, 1976).

13. See Irving R. Kaufman, "A Legal Remedy for International Torture," *New York Times Magazine* 52 (1980). The author, a judge of the United States Court of Appeals for the Second Circuit, wrote the opinion of the court.

14. Indeed, the primacy of these requirements is manifest even in the United Nations, which has thus far barred free access of states to secret files on 40,000 war criminals, suspects, and witnesses to atrocities during World War II. These files were collected from 1943 to 1948 by the United Nations War Crimes Commission in London. Although they represent the most comprehensive concentration of information concerning suspected and accused Nazi war criminals, these files remain inaccessible except for "United Nations purposes." Moreover, the extent of these files became known only after it was disclosed that a dossier charging former Secretary General Kurt Waldheim (now president of Austria) was in the archives. Waldheim is one of 24,500 individuals who were given an A classification, the commission's most serious, indicating that the subject should be tried. See "Israel Urges U.N. to Open War Files," *New York Times*, May 2, 1986, 10.

15. See David Hume, *A Treatise of Human Nature* (1739; reprint 1911), 195.

16. In an October 17, 1980, campaign statement, President Reagan denounced the "gross hypocrisy" of the Carter administration because it "supported the Pol Pot Communist Cambodian regime, which had slaughtered millions of its own people, in the United Nations." Yet the Reagan administration voted for several years to keep the deposed Pol Pot regime seated in the UN. Although a coalition was formed between Norodom Sihanouk, Son Sann, and Pol Pot's Democratic Kampuchea, only the latter has maintained significant military force. For important assessments of the U.S. role in the Cambodian genocide, see William Shawcross, *Sideshow: Kissinger, Nixon and the Destruction of Cambodia* (New York: Simon and Schuster, 1979); and, by the same author, *The Quality of Mercy: Cambodia, Holocaust and Modern Conscience* (New York: Simon and Schuster, 1984).

17. An example of using the domestic jurisdiction principle of the charter as a shield for such misconceived intuitions can be found in certain state reactions to Chinese genocide against Tibet in the 1950s. During this period, according to a report issued by the International Commission of Jurists (*The Question of Tibet and the Rule of Law*) in 1959, the Chinese killed tens of thousands of Tibetans; deported thousands of Tibetan children; killed Buddhist monks and lamas on a very large scale; and subjected religious leaders and public officials to forced labor, arbitrary arrest, and torture. The evidence pointed to "a systemic design to eradicate the separate national, cultural and religious life of Tibet." These facts notwithstanding, the East European socialist states (with the exception of Yugoslavia) acted as a solid bloc in defense of China, arguing that Tibet was an integral part of the People's Republic and that consideration of the question of Tibet by the UN General Assembly constituted an intervention in China's domestic affairs. For more on this matter, see Kuper, *The Prevention of Genocide*

158–59. See also Phuntsog Wangyal, "Tibet: A Case of Eradication of Religion Leading to Genocide," in *Toward the Understanding and Prevention of Genocide*, ed. Israel W. Charny, (Boulder, Colo.: Westview Press, 1984), 119–126.

18. Indeed, our very definitions of pathological behavior omit the most terrible crimes of unfeeling, including genocide. Using the definitions accepted in psychology and psychiatry, it is not necessarily pathological behavior to take part in mass murder or genocide. Eichmann and other major Nazi functionaries in the Holocaust were repeatedly described as "completely sane." This suggests, among other things, the triumph of the absurd, a world in which mass killers may be "normal," but where legions of harmless people who suffer mild neuroses and anxieties are characterized as "emotionally disturbed" or "mentally ill." For an exploration of this situation, which reveals just how far-reaching the absence of responsibility to others has become in contemporary life, see Israel W. Charny, "Genocide and Mass Destruction: Doing Harm to Others as a Missing Dimension in Psychopathology," *Psychiatry: Interpersonal and Biological Processes* 49, no. 2 (May 1986): 144–157.

19. See Thomas Paine, *Common Sense*, Introduction (February 14, 1776); reprinted in S. Hook, ed., *The Essential Thomas Paine* (New York: New American Library/Mentor, 1969), 23–24.

20. See Frances G. Grossman, "A Psychological Study of Gentiles Who Saved the Lives of Jews During the Holocaust," in *Toward the Understanding and Prevention of Genocide*, ed. Israel W. Charny, (Boulder, Colo.: Westview Press, 1984), 207. The Nazi killings illustrate the extent to which persons may transfer responsibility to others and even rationalize the transferrence in terms of the presumed obligations of legal and ethical imperatives. For example, in response to questioning at his trial in Jerusalem, Adolf Eichmann maintained that he had not only obeyed orders (at times identifying blind obedience as the "obedience of corpses," or *Kadavergehorsam*), but he had also obeyed the *law*. Moreover, he insisted that he had lived his entire life according to Kant's moral precepts, especially according to a Kantian definition of duty. Explaining that he had read Kant's *Critique of Practical Reason*, Eichmann identified his work toward "the final solution" in terms of an altered version of the categorical imperative. In Hannah Arendt's formulation: "Act in such a way that the Führer, if he knew your actions, would approve it." In Kant's philosophy, the source of law was practical reason; for Eichmann it was the will of the Führer. See Hannah Arendt, *Eichmann in Jerusalem: A Report on the Banality of Evil* (New York: Penguin, 1963), 136.

21. See G. S. Graber, *The History of the SS* (New York: David McKay, 1978), 144. See also Lucy S. Dawidowicz, *The War against the Jews, 1933–1945* (New York: Holt, Rinehart and Winston, 1975), 129.

22. See Philip Hallie, "Scepticism, Narrative and Holocaust Ethics," *The Philosophical Forum* 16, nos. 1–2 (Fall-Winter 1984–85): 38. For more on Le Chambon, see Philip Hallie, *Lest Innocent Blood Be Shed* (New York: Harper and Row, 1979).

23. The bewitchment of language, of course, reached its "highest" expression under the Nazis. In the lexicon of the Third Reich, words such as extermination, liquidation, and killing rarely surfaced. Rather, the goal was "final solution"

(*Endlosung*), and the prescribed methods involved "evacuation" (*Aussiedlung*), "special treatment" (*Sonderbehandlung*), and "resettlement" (*Umsiedlung*). Indeed, all communications regarding "final solution" were subject to a strict "language rule" (*Sprachregelung*) that was itself a perversion of language.

24. See Robert Jay Lifton, *The Life of the Self: Toward a New Psychology* (New York: Simon and Schuster, 1976), 111.

25. See Alan L. Berger, "Holocaust: The Pedagogy of Paradox," in *Toward the Understanding and Prevention of Genocide*, ed. Israel W. Charny, (Boulder, Colo.: Westview Press, 1984), 269.

26. The connection between an overriding interest in commercial profit and the practice of genocide is already a matter of historical record. Consider the following bids returned, in Nazi Germany, for the construction of gas chambers:

   1. A. Tops and Sons, Erfurt, manufacturers of heating equipment: "We acknowledge receipt of your order for five triple furnaces, including two electric elevators for raising the corpses and one emergency elevator."

   2. Vidier Works, Berlin: "For putting the bodies into the furnace, we suggest simply a metal fork moving on cylinders."

   3. C. H. Kori: "We guarantee the effectiveness of the cremation ovens, as well as their durability, the use of the best material and our faultless workmanship."

   See Harry H. Shapiro, "A Search for Conscience," *Philadelphia Jewish Exponent*, March 29, 1968; cited in Israel W. Charny, *How Can We Commit the Unthinkable? Genocide: The Human Cancer* (Boulder, Colo.: Westview Press, 1982), 185.

27. See Ernest Becker, *Escape from Evil* (New York: Free Press, 1975), 81–82.

28. This idea has been captured with particular insight by Eugene Ionesco in his "Diaries": "I must kill my visible enemy, the one who is determined to take my life, to prevent him from killing me. Killing gives me a feeling of relief, because I am dimly aware that in killing him, I have killed death. . . . Killing is a way of relieving one's feelings, of warding off one's own death." See also the illuminating explanations in Israel W. Charny, *How Can We Commit the Unthinkable? Genocide: The Human Cancer.*

7

The United States and Peace: A Possible Future in Retrospect

"I N a dark time," says the poet Theodore Roethke, "the eye begins to see." During the last twenty years (1990–2010), America has begun to erect durable structures of peace. Spurred on by the irresistible challenge of a vast chaos from which there could be neither escape nor sanctuary, our nation has launched a global ark of renewal. Rejecting the desolate precepts of power politics, it has embraced a new pattern of thinking, one based on the affirmation of reason and planetary identity.

Before 1990, the nations of the world had abandoned themselves to the instant, to self-induced encounters with despair. By the end of the 1980s, approximately forty major and minor conflicts were underway in the world. With over four million soldiers directly engaged in combat, the estimated loss of life to date in these conflicts approached five million. UN Secretary General Javier Perez de Cuellar warned that the world was "perilously near to a new international anarchy."

Every minute, thirty children died for want of food and inexpensive vaccines while, every minute, the world's military budget absorbed $1.3 million.

The cost of a single new nuclear submarine equaled the annual education budget of twenty-three developing countries with 160 million school-age children.

The planet's stockpile of nuclear weapons represented an explosive force over 5000 times greater than all the munitions used in World War II.

At the close of President Reagan's second term, this world stood close to the margins of existence. Continuing their adherence to social Darwinism in global affairs, the nations of planet Earth moved toward widening insecurity, growing poverty, greater injustice, and ecological collapse. Overshadowing all of these aspects of danger and decay was the unique threat of nuclear war.

The Reagan administration seemed not to notice. Indeed, it appeared insistent on compounding its errors:

> Continuing the "logic" that peace flows from successful competition in an arms race rather than from arms control, the administration ceased compliance with the SALT II Treaty. Although this treaty was never ratified by the U.S. Senate, both superpowers had agreed to act as if it were actually in force.

> Convinced that antisatellite controls were unverifiable, the administration acknowledged no alternative to an arms race in space. Although this position ran counter to the findings of the Union of Concerned Scientists and other reputable groups of experts, which claimed that adequate verification was possible, the president denounced talks that might have led to a treaty on limiting weapons to destroy orbiting satellites. Naturally the Pentagon then pressed forward with development of an antisatellite missile system.

> Committed to a provocative force of Euromissiles that could destroy the Soviet homeland in less than ten minutes of flight time, the administration refused to halt deployment. As a result, the Soviets accelerated their own deployment of intermediate-range nuclear forces. The Reagan administration position was especially ironic since none of the Pershing II or ground-launched cruise missiles could ever have been used in retaliation for conventional attack by a sane and rational U.S. president.

> Tantalized by the promise of a new counterforce, nuclear-warfighting weapon, the administration continued with its plan to deploy MX (The Peacekeeper) before determining whether the missiles or their silos could work properly. Once again, there

was considerable irony in this move since the MX could do nothing to improve U.S. deterrence. It could only refine and enlarge America's capacity to fight a nuclear war so that we might "prevail."

Believing that there could be adequate defense against a nuclear attack, the administration proceeded with its plan for a "Star Wars" technology (involving directed-energy weapons such as lasers and particle beams, optical and other means of pointing the beams accurately, high-speed data processing for battle control, methods of placing such equipment in space, and space-based mirrors to reflect ground lasers). It proceeded with this technology although virtually the entire scientific community in this country rejected the idea of an umbrella against Soviet missile attack. Indeed, the administration spent at least $26 billion through 1988 even though the Pentagon itself had not recognized the feasibility of high-degree protection for the American civilian population. The attempt to go ahead with Star Wars violated existing arms control agreements, especially the ABM Treaty.

Buttressed by its hopes for Star Wars technologies, advanced ballistic missile defense, and air defense, the administration stepped up its plans for civil defense of the nation's population. Supported by $4.2 billion in budget authority, these plans called for the "temporary relocation" of approximately 150 million people from about 400 "high risk" metropolitan and defense-related areas to about 2,000 allegedly safer "host areas" during periods when nuclear attack appeared imminent. There was absolutely no reason to believe that such relocation would ever work (in New York City evacuation was to take place largely by subway) or that it could protect even a tiny fraction of our population from the effects of a "nuclear winter." As the Federal Emergency Management Agency (the federal agency charged with statutory responsibility on these matters) itself admitted, if the Soviet Union were to mount an all-out attack on the United States, "almost the whole population would be located less than 100 miles of at least one nuclear detonation." This meant that (1) virtually every American would be within range of serious fallout radiation exposure; and (2) almost half the U.S. population would experience direct weapons effects.

It was an American farewell to arms control. Considering not only SALT, but the entire edifice of formal arms control negotiations as an obsolete remnant of the 1970s, the Reagan administration re-dedicated itself to the time-dishonored traditions of realpolitik. While the Kremlin made overtures to stabilize superpower relations, Washington resisted on every front.

During 1986 Mikhail S. Gorbachev offered (1) a comprehensive set of arms control proposals (January 15); (2) a reduction in offensive missiles in return for a renewed mutual commitment to a strict construction of the Anti-Ballistic Missile Treaty (which would confine Star Wars to the laboratory for fifteen years); and (3) an extended (four times) unilateral moratorium on nuclear testing. Ronald Reagan's response was to continue with the uninterruped building of nuclear and related forms of weapons. In the words of Townsend Hoopes, a former undersecretary of the U.S. Air Force, the administration was making every effort to misrepresent Gorbachev's "constructive proposals" and to "conceal the truth of its own purpose, which is to dismantle all remaining pieces of the arms control structure in order to clear the decks for an unrestricted arms race on earth and in space." Indeed, continued Hoopes, the president's policies were "driven by Pentagon civilians whose only vision is nuclear superiority, whose fascination is with the fine-tuning of nuclear warfighting strategies and whose preferred method is to run the arms race to infinity, unfettered by treaty restrictions."[1]

At the heart of the president's farewell to arms control was his obsessive fantasy of Star Wars, a vision of Fortress America in the space age, an orbital variant of the Sixth Fleet.

Star Wars had its appeal. Its supporters asked only that we give new technologies a chance. What they failed to understand was that the stability of nuclear deterrence rested on mutual vulnerability. An ambitious program to prevent the other side's "assured destruction capability" was enormously *offensive*. Ironically, this should have been obvious to everyone who remembered that the MIRVed Soviet weapons that once threatened us were developed originally to penetrate an earlier generation of ABM (anti-ballistic missile) defenses.

President Reagan told us that since Star Wars would be entirely defensive, the Soviets had nothing to fear. But in this assessment he displayed a near-total misunderstanding of nuclear deterrence. Significantly, if the Soviets had embarked on the "defensive" system then being planned in Washington, this country would have responded with a greatly accelerated deployment of offensive missile systems—nuclear weapons that could have reliably penetrated the Soviet shield.

The main problem with the president's reasoning was that it ignored Soviet uncertainty. Notwithstanding his assurances of America's peaceful intentions, there was little cause for complacence in Moscow. From the Soviet perspective, everything pointed to U.S. flirtation with a disarming first-strike, especially as our plan for strategic defense was coupled with the ongoing deployment of MX, Trident II, and Euromissiles—a deployment with distinctly "counterforce" or war-fighting qualities.

The president told us that it was time to shift from deterrence to defense, but no such shift was possible. The development of Star Wars could never replace nuclear deterrence, it could only destabilize it.

The president told us that the Soviets need have no fears of a U.S. first strike. Everyone knew that we were "good" and they were "bad."

But it didn't look that way from the Soviet point of view:

They saw a United States that was the only country to have used nuclear weapons.

They saw a United States that had refused to renounce (as they had renounced) the right to "first use" of nuclear weapons.

They saw a United States that refused to ratify the SALT II treaty and then had the gall to accuse them of noncompliance.

They saw a United States that had surrounded their country with 572 new (Pershing II and ground-launched cruise) missiles.

The president told us that Star Wars could work and that the Soviets were less likely to attack if we had such defense, even if it were imperfect. Yet according to all that we knew about the logic of deterrence, their judgment on whether to attack first would have depended on (1) expectations of retaliatory destruction and (2) expectations of American preemption.

If all of our cities were completely vulnerable, a rational Soviet adversary would never have struck first unless it believed it could do so without suffering unacceptably damaging retaliation. Under such conditions the Soviets would have had no cause for concern about U.S. preemption.

Conversely, if all our cities were completely defensible, the Soviets might have decided to strike first if they believed they could do so without suffering assured destruction. Their concern over a U.S. first strike under such conditions would have been enormous.

Whether or not the Soviets would gain from striking first depended entirely on their views of American intentions. Because Star Wars signaled a search for defense, it suggested a greatly enhanced prospect of a U.S. first-strike. Thus it could only have enlarged the chances that the Soviets would preempt, a conclusion totally opposite to administration arguments.

The president did not understand the calculus of nuclear deterrence. Recognizing that each side could "assuredly destroy" the other after absorbing a first-strike, he concluded falsely that American safety would be reinforced by strategic defense. But there are circumstances in which striking first would have been the rational Soviet choice, however damaging the expected retaliation. These are circumstances in which the only perceived Soviet alternative to striking first would have been to be struck first. *Since defense would create these circumstances, Star Wars greatly undermined our national security.*

These facts notwithstanding, Star Wars still had its supporters. Some went along for strongly personal economic reasons. Star Wars smelled of money; the public be damned. Still, after a time, everyone would have discovered that the crayon lines so neatly drawn on TV commercials for Star Wars did not prevent oblivion. Looking up at the moment of truth, we would have learned that Star Wars had saved no one, not even the investors, engineers, and defense contractors who grew fat before the final battle.

Some who favored Star Wars were driven by the visceral anti-Sovietism of the time. Unwilling to work through the complex logical arguments associated with Star Wars, they retreated to the vacant intuitions of armchair warriors, comforted not by wisdom but by dogma. Incapable of serious thought, they attempted to discredit the other side's position by invoking colorful metaphors and patriotic fervor.

But their views did not prevail. After Mikhail Gorbachev extended, for the fourth time, his unilateral test moratorium, new doubts about President Reagan's malingering approach to arms control began to surface. Why, Americans asked, had the Russians not conducted a weapons test since August 6, 1985, while during the same period the United States had conducted sixteen such tests? Why was the moratorium so disadvantageous to us when at the start of the Soviet moratorium the United States was believed to have conducted 803 nuclear tests compared to 604 Soviet tests? Why didn't the Soviets have the same need for "proof testing" their weapons that President Reagan insisted was essential to maintain the reliability of weapons already in our stockpile? Why did President Reagan refuse even to negotiate for a comprehensive test ban treaty, the only American president to take such a stand since Dwight D. Eisenhower announced the first test moratorium in 1958?

These questions were on everybody's mind when a successor to Mr. Reagan was elected in 1988. The new president began to match the awesome agenda of world order reform with purposeful strategies of response.

Taking the lead from the 100,000 members of the Union of Concerned Scientists, he pledged: (1) immediate reinstatement of SALT II (recognizing its ceiling on strategic weapons as the essential baseline for deep cuts in both American and Soviet nuclear arsenals); (2) immediate strengthening of the Anti-Ballistic Missile Treaty to ensure that testing of ABM components in space would be prohibited and to resolve ambiguities related to Star Wars, radar arrays, and antisatellite weapons; and (3) immediate work toward a comprehensive ban on nuclear tests.

Starting with the American president's initiatives on nuclear arms control—initiatives involving the end of Euromissile deployments, cessation of Star Wars, a comprehensive test ban, and a treaty prohibiting antisatellite weapons in space—a pattern for superpower cooperation was established.

When the Soviets responded with parallel concessions, the United States also accepted the requirements of a nuclear freeze and a no-first-use policy. This was followed by joint U.S.-Soviet implementation of additional nuclear-weapon-free zones and by a continuous, staged, bilateral removal of the most destabilizing weapons. Without compromising the survivability of either side's "assured destruction" capability, missiles having multiple warheads were phased out in favor of smaller, single-warhead missiles. By this change each side was able to reduce its fear of a preemptive attack. During the past several years we have entered into the final phases of arms control and disarmament, beginning the physical destruction of all remaining stockpiles of nuclear weapons.

The freeze, which banned the testing, production, and deployment of all new missiles with multiple warheads, was not the first step in the deescalatory initiative. But its move to end the deployment of weapons with "counterforce" or warfighting capability greatly reduced pressure on leaders to launch first in a crisis or to move toward postures of "launch-on-warning." Together with a "build-down" formula that allowed progress toward single-warhead missiles without creating new uncertainties, the freeze was a vital precondition to our current success.

Although some had argued that a freeze would only codify a condition of American military inferiority, the new president knew better. At the time, a careful analysis by the International Institute for Strategic Studies—considered by experts to be the most authoritative independent source of data on world military forces—described superpower arsenals as essentially equal. Even more importantly, since the concepts of superiority and inferiority are of limited significance in matters of nuclear deterrence, it was understood that a freeze could not jeopardize this country's capacity to deliver "unacceptably damaging" retaliation.

Without a freeze, the president knew that it would have become increasingly difficult for each side to keep track of the arms race. Soon it would have become impossible to monitor weapons developments with any degree of reliability, a situation that would have generated new incentives to strike first. Moreover, the chances for an accidental nuclear war would have been enlarged.

Looking back, it is clear that a most critical element of the arms control process was one that went beyond the progressive reduction and elimination of weapons. This element was the transformation of foreign policy objectives. Recognizing the interrelatedness of their national destinies, the leaders of the United States, the Soviet Union, and all of the other major powers began to seek a new definition of national interest.

Turning away from the impersonal logic of possessive individualism, these leaders sought more enduring patterns of safety—patterns that were in harmony with the true imperatives of national and international life. They found these patterns in the idea of planetary consciousness and responsibility. By building on the understanding that it was in each state's best interest to develop its foreign policy from a common vantage point, they created the kind of global renaissance that was so desperately needed, a renaissance that "spilled over" into reduced levels of terrorism and genocide.

How exactly was this able to happen? First, the American president took a cue from the warning in George Washington's farewell address that "the nation which indulges toward another an habitual hatred . . . is in some degree a slave." Rather than persist in the inclination to describe U.S.-Soviet rivalry as a death struggle between the Sons of Light and the Sons of Darkness—an inclination that only undermined our national interest—he proceeded to act on the basis of a *shared value* in preserving peace.

Second, the president took great pains to see the world from the Soviet point of view. Remembering what had happened to the Soviet Union in June 1941, he recognized the unusually provocative nature of Pershing II missiles in West Germany. Coupled with the understanding that these missiles degraded deterrence by contributing to Soviet fears of a U.S. first strike, this sensitivity to recent history led to the withdrawal of Euromissiles.

Third, the president understood that the rivalry between the superpowers, once spawned and sustained by genuine considerations of purpose and power, had become essentially a contrivance. Contrary to what everyone had always believed without question, the underlying point of contention between the United States and the USSR was no longer ideological or economic but a self-fulfilling and groundless rhetoric. Indeed, in what was perhaps the greatest single irony of modern world politics, the military communities of both countries were the only true allies, supporting each other's calls for "rearmament" while they corroded the security of both countries.

By 1990 it had become apparent that Soviet foreign policy drew no more nourishment from Marx and Lenin than did ours from Washington and Jefferson. For a time Marxism-Leninism had been a catechism that everyone recited but no one believed. But with the abandonment of endless varieties of Marxist scholasticism that had been fashionable in European universities, even the recitations disappeared. The Kremlin acted for the Russian state, nothing more. Ignoring the canonical version of its public orthodoxy, the Soviet Union acted much like the Czarist regime in foreign affairs. As was observed by Octavio Paz: "As is always the case, this policy is dictated by geography, the mother of history; it is also a continuation of an expansionist imperial tradition. In the past, the ideology that supported this expansionism was Pan-Slavism; today it is Marxism-Leninism."[2]

Recognizing that each society's claims for a better world order were merely pretexts for a *Pax Americana* or a *Pax Sovietica*, the American president portrayed these claims as the crippling metaphysic of his time. Although the superpowers had been arming against each other, their immediate victims included the rest of the world. The cold war, in the words of George Konrad, had become "the new Holy Alliance." According to Konrad: "Bipolar power forces societies to submit to the discipline of one bloc or the other and to varying—significantly varying—degrees of paternalism and force. Two different types of hierarchical system weigh upon society, and their ultimate police sanction is the machinery of war, which in the last analysis means atomic weapons. The Soviet bomb guarantees the police discipline of the West; the American bomb guarantees the police discipline of the East."[3]

When the American president began to act on a higher form of international understanding, his immediate concern was to control the "vertical" arms race between the superpowers. In so doing, however, he also strengthened the nonproliferation regime. Fulfilling the agreement that had been struck between nuclear and nonnuclear weapon states at Article 6 of the Nonproliferation Treaty—a treaty that entered into force in 1970—the United States and the Soviet Union were able to generate a far-reaching pattern of imitation and reciprocity. Consequently, the spread of nuclear weapons to other countries was halted by the early 1990s.

When he first began his peace initiative, the American president was criticized from certain sectors within the country. How, he was asked repeatedly, could he expect us to survive in a world of international anarchy without waging a relentless military struggle for existence? How did he expect us to endure in a menacing cold war without keeping up competition in the implements of violence?

His answer was momentous. *"Violence,"* he told us, *"was not power. Poised at the edge of history, we must infuse our foreign policy with a new understanding of partnership, with the Soviet Union and with the entire family of nations."*

With this statement the president began to underscore the total uselessness of a nuclear threat system. Sloughing off the shackles of outmoded forms of self-interest, he offered a set of policies that extended the principles of superpower war avoidance to the rest of international society. The centerpiece of this universal regime was the cosmopolitan view that all states, like all people, form one essential body and one true community. This view, that a latent oneness lay buried beneath the manifold divisions of a fractionated world, was not based on the mythical attractions of spontaneous brotherhood, but on the incontestable connection between survival and relatedness.

The false dichotomy of East and West had made clear thinking impossible. Tired of thinking in clichés, the president left ideological warfare to the apparatchiks and to universities swollen with intellectuals for hire. Instead he acknowledged democracy as the overriding value of all political life. In this he reflected the view of George Konrad: "I am neither a communist nor an anticommunist, neither a capitalist nor an anticapitalist; if one must absolutely be for or against something, I consider a permanently open democracy to be the greatest good, and the ideological war that constantly casts the shadow of atomic war on the wall to be the greatest evil. Ideological war speaks a language of sensationalism; on all sides it continually stuffs minds meant for better things full of lies and half-truths."[4]

Several years before the president's initiative, a prominent historian of that period, Barbara W. Tuchman, had defined *folly* as "perverse persistence in a policy demonstrably unworkable or counterproductive." Whether or not the president had read *The March of Folly* we can only speculate, but one thing is clear: He understood completely that continued reliance on the threat and use of military force for security, especially nuclear weapons, was pure folly.

Looking back, it is difficult to see how anyone might have disagreed with such an understanding. Since the stockpiled nuclear weapons in existence at that time could have killed all life permanently, the consequences of a nuclear war might have been omnicide.

Killing not only life, but life-giving death, nuclear war could have destroyed not only all of nature but even the natural relation of death to life.

It is now also easy to recognize that the concept of a balance of power was a groundless basis for optimism about avoiding a nuclear war. Never actually durable, never more than a clever metaphor, this concept had nothing to do with genuine equilibrium. Since it was always a matter of individual perceptions, neither side ever really believed that strategic conditions were balanced. Each side feared that it was always a little bit behind. Thus the net effect of the search for balance was inevitably disequilibrium and insecurity.

Faced with the possibility of a remorseless judgment—a judgment in which death would take place without rebirth—the president decided to *take a chance*. There were no guarantees that his initiatives would work. Yet he understood that there were no reasonable alternatives, as the risks of unreciprocated U.S. moves toward minimum deterrence and denuclearization were very low compared to the risks of expanded nuclear competition. Quoting C. P. Snow, the English physicist and writer, the president commented: "On the one side, we have a finite risk. On the other side, we have certainty of disaster. Between a risk and a certainty, a sane man does not hesitate."

To a considerable extent, the president's initiative also drew on the corrosive effects of high levels of military spending on the civilian economy. Tied up in an enormously expensive competition with the Soviet Union, the United States had lost status and competitiveness in commercial markets. Significantly, in 1990 the United States and the USSR—first in the capacity to wreak military destructiveness (as distinguished from first in the capacity to exercise real *power*)— ranked far from the top in ordinary measures of economic-social standing. Recognizing and *feeling* this, millions of Americans began to reject the false "bargain" extended by the herd.

By accelerating its commitment to military priorities at the expense of social and economic needs, the United States had retarded its development through inflation, diversion of investment, misuse of scarce materials, and misuse of human capital. Small wonder, then, that the president of Columbia University spoke of disquieting developments wherein "the per capita gross national product of the U.S. has slipped to tenth place in the world" and where "our foreign trade pattern resembles that of an underdeveloped country." Largely because of the consequences of its debilitating pattern of military spending, the United States had exported raw materials in abundance and imported more manufactured goods than it sold abroad. The result was a society less and less able to provide its citizens with improved conditions of living. Ironically, this result was accompanied by a steady decline in security from foreign attack and by an expanded willingness to seek self-worth from *within*.

In taking his initiatives, the president offered another far-reaching change. This change involved a return of individual human dignity, rather than state power, to center stage in world affairs. It was a change that reversed the predatory advance of realpolitik that had been underway for several hundred years.

By the middle of the twentieth century the state had assumed its own rationale. Holding its will as preeminent, it had become a sacred phenomenon, intent upon sacrificing private interests and personal lives at the altar of global power competition. A stand-in for God, it was a providence of which everything was accepted and nothing expected.

The problem of the omnivorous state had been forseen brilliantly in the 1930s by José Ortega y Gasset. In his *Revolt of the Masses*, Ortega correctly identified the state "as the greatest danger," mustering its immense and unassailable resources "to crush beneath it any creative minority which disturbs it." Set in motion by individuals whom it had already rendered anonymous, the state established its machinery above society so that humankind came to live for the state.

Anticipating the encroachment of unbearable circumstances, a vanguard of informed and transformed Americans led to the president's initiatives. Challenging the wizards of realpolitik on their unfounded pretensions to expertise, these individuals acknowledged the imperative to survive. Defied again and again by the banal syntax of power politics, they were prepared to support the president in his last-minute disengagement from irrationality and war.

Nuclear deterrence had not yet failed, but it was a serious disease; a semiparalysis of the soul. The "experts" had persisted in warnings about "appeasement" and the need for "peace through strength," but we recognized their intense, multisyllabic jabs of speech as the words of fools. Intrepidly incorrect, these "realists" instructed us to take heart from the cold, metallic surface of the state, but the stale scent of the coming world war could not be ignored. It was cadaverous.

We rejected the glib, smug preachings of the experts and the foolish optimism of a society approaching extinction, but not entirely because of an outpouring of reason. By itself, intellect is often impotent against even the most palpable nonsense,[5] and falsehood must be revealed through another power—the power of personhood. This power emerged only because a collapsing civilization revealed the desolation of society, a revelation that made possible our rejection of the state as the highest source of meaning.

The swaying of the ship was so violent that even the best-hung lamps were overturned. We became aware that America displayed the same fragility as an individual life, and that only by caring for ourselves as persons could we care for our country. We learned that the visible earth is made of ashes, and that ashes signify something. Through the obscure depths of history we could make out the phantoms of great ships of state laden with riches and intellect. We could not count them, but we understood that the disasters that had sent them down *were* our affair. We learned the meaning of the lines written by Paul Valery in 1919: "The circumstances that could send the works of Keats and Baudelaire to join the works of Menander are no longer inconceivable; they are in the newspapers."[6]

We lived in a twilight era. Faced with the end of this world, we understood the responsibility to be *in* the world, to act *in* history. Unwilling to accept abolition of the future, we rescued life from the twin threats of petrifaction and explosion.

Something preceded this fortunate turn of events. Acknowledging the vulgarity of our captivity by endless cycles of useless production and consumption, we began to move toward meaningful definitions of personhood. Rejecting the relentless docility of the crowd, we discarded artificial definitions of wealth in favor of true private and national growth.

It was almost as if Plato were being taken seriously. Abhorred by what he termed *pleonexia*—the hunger for more and more—Plato understood the hazards that lie latent in deformed measures of progress. Exceeding and destroying all measure, such hunger (because measure or correct proportion is the standard of both public and private health) leads directly to corruption and death.

Inventiveness took new forms. Revolted by the mob and its mouthpieces, we began to understand our disorder. A collapsing civilization compromises with its disease, cherishes the infectious pathogen. We, however, chose to fight, attacking the false communion of social and political life with wisdom and understanding.

"The wrinkles of a nation," wrote E. M. Cioran in *The Temptation to Exist*, "are as visible as those of an individual." Witnessing the dying reflexes of the United States, we trembled at the visible manifestations of America's aggressions against itself. After so much imposture, so much fraud, we had enough. Engulfed by the refined gobbledygook of state and society, we were transformed.

Twenty years ago, in 1990, international relations—despite their veneer of civility and wise purpose—were based on a profane seduction. Lured by the siren calls of power and domination, states had reduced individuals to feeble specks surrounded by unfathomable depths of silence. Proud of their ethical illiteracy, because it suggested cold and considered strategic calculations, governments were in fact the champions of unreason. Intrigued by their own mendacities of language, they failed to recognize themselves as bearers not of safety but of ruin and fatality.

Yet faced with stark intimations of their vulnerability, Americans acknowledged the responsibility to endure. As a result the once prevailing drift to sanctify states has been reversed. Although the prospect of such a reversal once appeared hopelessly utopian, it is now apparent that the truest forms of realism lay in the imaginings of idealists, imaginings that carried within themselves the seeds of their own verification.

Twenty years ago the world stood face to face with the hour of its own death. Perhaps because the perversion of human ingenuity through nuclear war would have represented the final triumph of meaninglessness, this dreadful confrontation became a time for planetary renewal. Instead of extinction with insignificance, humankind rejected the humiliating delusions of realpolitik in favor of lucidity. Avoiding nuclear war, until then only a marginal tic of consciousness, became an irreversible gesture.

To survive, the United States learned to recognize that the Soviet Union had much to gain from a mutual and graduated process of deescalation and conflict reduction. Although this country continued, in the early stages, to ensure the survivability of its strategic triad, this objective was satisfied while reversing a search for expanded counterforce capabilities and expanded theater nuclear force deployments. Having reached that point in human evolution where it becomes possible to recognize gigantic failures, this country was able to escape collective disintegration.

In the words of Ecclesiasticus, "Vain hopes delude the senseless and dreams give wings to a fool's fancy." These words acquired a special meaning in the repudiation of earlier plans to fight and "prevail" in a nuclear war. Having taken civilization seriously, an enlarged body of conscious individuals stood before the purveyors of strategic myth, countering their vaporous effrontery with prudence and understanding. In so doing they gave new meaning to Samuel Beckett's question: "What is the good of passing from one untenable position to another, of seeking justification always on the same plane?"

This meaning concerned the futility of seeking peace through unending refinements of nuclear overkill. Twenty years ago more than 50,000 nuclear weapons, carrying explosive power equivalent to more than 1 million Hiroshima bombs, existed on earth. This amounted to more than 13 billion tons of TNT, more than 3 tons for every man, woman, and child.

America had been thinking against itself. To avoid fatal contamination by the supersitions of realpolitik, it learned to resist confronting the apocalypse as healer. Its sole ambition was to prevent the incurable.

The realpolitiker's premise that nuclear disaster could not befall the United States represented a potentially fatal flight from reality. The dinosaurs ruled this planet for millions of years, far longer than the brief tenure of our own species. And they are gone, leaving nothing but crushed bones.

Twenty years ago our only hope for survival lay in facing squarely the possibilities of a nuclear winter. To transform their primal terrors into constructive attempts at prevention, the president and an informed public responded not with paralysis but with productive action. In response, the problems of realpolitik became increasingly obvious.

A few years after the Declaration of Independence, the Continental Congress adopted as a motto on the great seal of the United States Virgil's phrase *Novus Ordo Seclorum* (A new age beginning). In a world imperiled by nuclear war, this motto came to be applied to American foreign policy. In a world where convulsive changes in technology signaled the possibility of gigadeath, or death in the billions, this country was able to substitute the dignity of cooperative international interaction for the tragedy of unlimited military competition. By its actions to make such substitution possible, the United States was able to confront the cataclysmic changes of an era not as a victim but as a gifted creator.

How did it happen? How did we grasp a new calculus of potentiality, reaffirming the sovereignty of personhood over the forces of war? How did rational thought (what Plato called *phronesis*) take a leading part?

Significantly, the myths of realpolitik and anti-Sovietism were not destroyed directly. There was never a frontal assault on these sources of our misfortune. Rather, they were undermined via far-reaching efforts at personal and social transformation. Politics came last. Before our policies could change, our society had to change. Before we could divert our disastrous course in world affairs, our citizens had to understand that their pursuit of power and pleasure could produce only unhappiness.

Plato understood this more than 2,000 years ago. The well-being of the polity inevitably depends on the well-being of its citizens. And the well-being of citizens is determined not by illusions of military superiority but by virtue. To create a viable polity, we had first to change a deformed and mean-spirited communal life. As Plato warned in his *Gorgias*, we needed to learn that our only purposeful objective lay in "making the souls of the citizens better."

The effects were striking. But they were incremental. The Talmud tells us, "The dust from which the first man was made was gathered in all the corners of the world." Although we have yet to grasp the full meaning of this wisdom, we are at last moving toward a generous new spirit of planetary identity. Shorn of our mistaken pretensions to provide peace through nuclear terror, we have learned to develop our capacity for cohesion with others to ever more distant boundaries.

We must now aim for something once thought impossible: a collaborative vision sparked by the impulse of human singularity. With the manifestation of the one in the many,[7] states may complete their commitment to planetization. In so doing, they can draw on the animating insight of Pierre Teilhard de Chardin: "The egocentric ideal of a future reserved for those who have managed to attain egoistically the extremity of 'everyone for himself' is false and against nature. No element could move and grow except with and by all others with itself."

Notes

1. See Townsend Hoopes, "Mr. Reagan's Myopia on Arms Control," *New York Times*, September 7, 1986, EY29.
2. See Octavio Paz, *One Earth, Four or Five Worlds: Reflections on Contemporary History*, trans. Helen R. Lane (New York: Harcourt Brace Jovanovich, 1985), 69–70.
3. See George Konrad, *Antipolitics*, trans. Richard E. Allen (New York: Harcourt Brace Jovanovich, 1984), 32–33.
4. Ibid., 35.
5. On this point, see C. G. Jung, *Psychology and Religion* (New Haven, Conn.: Yale University Press, 1938).
6. Taken from Paul Valery, "The Crisis of the Mind" (1919) in *Paul Valery: An Anthology*, ed. James R. Lawler (London: Routledge and Kegan Paul, 1977), 94.
7. In a passage of his dialogue *Theatetus*, Plato compares Greek philosophy to a battlefield on which two great armies meet in incessant combat. On the one side are the partisans of the "Many," on the other the partisans of the "One."

8

Selfhood and U.S. Foreign Policy: Toward a New Synthesis

W E have seen that the core problem of U.S. foreign policy lies in the behavior of individuals. Before we can begin to escape from the fatal limitations of obsessive anti-Sovietism, individual Americans will need to discover authentic bases of status and self-worth. To continue to survive, we cannot draw our meaning from membership in a crowd.

For the moment, America needs to despise the Soviet Union because such hatred reaffirms goodness in the United States. The value of our crowd is established dialectically by the evil of another crowd. In a sense, America loves to hate the Soviet Union because the Evil Empire guarantees the potency of the Free World, and doubts cast upon the devil undermine faith in God.

Yet if Americans could draw meaning as individuals, we would not need to cultivate hatred of the Soviet Union. Reconstructing ourselves on the ruins of crowd theology, we could begin to distance ourselves from loyalties that acknowledge only self-contempt, loyalties that demand hatred and ultimately oblivion. Such imagination could result in a new and auspicious U.S. foreign policy, one that would liberate this country from its incessant preparations for the apocalypse and from the presumed obligation to selectively oppose human rights in the interests of "freedom."

Consider the possibilities! In its direct relations with the Soviet Union, America could take real steps to end the nuclear arms race.

As described earlier in this book, the president of the United States could end Euromissile deployments and Star Wars and initiate a comprehensive test ban and a treaty prohibiting antisatellite weapons in space. In response, the Soviets could offer parallel concessions, which in turn could occasion a joint nuclear freeze and no-first-use agreement. All this could be followed by joint implementation of additional nuclear-weapon-free zones and by a continuous, staged, bilateral removal of the most destabilizing weapons.

In its indirect relations with the Soviet Union, America could progress beyond policies of support for "authoritarian" regimes and opposition to "totalitarian" ones that now produce endless humiliations. In South Africa, when apartheid is overthrown, the successor black majority government could turn to the United States as an ally rather than adversary. In consequence the United States could forgo the kinds of lawless insurgencies that it has directed against states such as Cuba and Nicaragua, insurgencies that have degraded our influence as they have blemished our ideals.

In Central America we could begin to retreat from repeated incursions that block the region from its own aspirations and that brand the United States as an international outlaw. When the contras are defeated, Nicaragua (because the United States will have ended its support of the terrorists) will not remain an enemy of our country. When repressive or even genocidal regimes are overthrown in Chile, Paraguay, and El Salvador, the new leadership in those countries (because the United States will have ended its support of authoritarian rule) will not feel obligated to join an expanding legion of anti-American states. The United States, long regarded in the region as an affliction, as the archetype of undemocratic counterrevolution, could become reidentified with the revolutionary principles of its Founding Fathers.

In the Middle East we could put an end to incomprehensible policies of intervention (for example, arms sales to Iran in 1986) that undermine our power and our safety from terrorism as they solidify our disrepute. We could begin to act as if the control of nuclear weapons in that region were of overriding interest to national and international security, action that could elicit Soviet cooperation in worldwide antiproliferation progress. Prior progress in controlling the "vertical" arms race between the superpowers (also a consequence of our personal and national retreat from pathological anti-

Sovietism) would be essential to preventing a rising pattern of nuclearization in the Middle East.

All of these possibilities depend on an end to our domination by the herd. The task, then, is for each American to become an individual. What exactly should be done? How can the essential discoveries take place? What steps must be taken on the path to becoming a person?

A good place to begin our inquiry is with the Faust legend.[1] The adjective *Faustian* is not easily defined but has certain commonly held meanings. For one, it signifies a continuing and restive striving, a search for the fullest and most profound appreciation of human existence. It also signifies a willingness to pursue this search at all costs.

This appears to be a dilemma. One's search for maximal individual development may run counter to community well-being. This dilemma, of course, revolves about the centuries-old discordance between the benefits of unfettered personal growth and the demands of interpersonal harmony. Too often, as Freud and others have pointed out, an irremediable antagonism is created between the search for personal progression and the obligations of social interaction.

The individual must learn to steer a steady course between the sheer rock of Scylla and the whirlpool of Charybdis, between the fully egoistic pole of private development and the personally destructive condition of social accord at any price. One must perpetually cultivate a sense of personal affirmation, but one must avoid unrestrained egotism. Goethe intended such egotism as Faust's undoing, and there is lasting wisdom in his meaning for students of U.S. foreign policy: Individual striving must be tempered by an ongoing concern for its additive effects. Where these effects are markedly antisocial, striving has exceeded its proper bounds.

How then can one achieve true fulfillment and avoid excessive self-centeredness? How must we strive if in striving we must err? Surely there is enormous pretense in venturing an answer, as Faust himself understood:

> I don't imagine I know anything worth while;
> I don't suppose I can teach anything
> To improve or convert the race of man.

But enormous promise is also wrapped up in the effort. And there is no lack of places to begin. A suitable starting point is Goethe's dictum that an individual must transcend himself and go on to become something unique. This growth of consciousness defines the key to our survival as a nation.

Of course, it is by transcending the limits of the herd and becoming a person that an individual can best contribute to the community. One can satisfy the demands of interpersonal harmony not by fitting in with the crowd but by self-consciously drawing meaning from the *inside*. Only then will an appropriate transformation of self and state be possible.

The crowd of statehood has always been false, but it needn't remain false forever. By seeking themselves within states, individuals can make these states seek genuine coexistence with all other states. Individuals' attachment to states can thus be transformed from counterfeit searches for meaning into self-affirming expressions of concern for all others.

A wondrous statement on this matter may be found in Richard Bach's *Jonathan Livingston Seagull*. This well-known parable about a seagull learning aerobatics is a potent portrayal of Goethe's dictum. In his incessant quest for perfection, Jonathan learns the true meaning of transcending oneself.

Jonathan discovers himself as a creature of excellence. He learns the meaning and importance of redefining the limits of his potential. He learns that the progressive awakening of consciousness to an ever-widening area of productive activity offers incomparable measures of satisfaction.

He also learns, to his consternation and dismay, that others of his kind do not easily share his newly discovered sense of purpose and perfection. Indeed, his one great sorrow is not solitude, but the fact that the other gulls "refused to believe the glory of flight that awaited them; they refused to open their eyes and see." If transformation is to have as a motif the emergence and growth of consciousness, we cannot expect an immediate opening to the fullness of vision.

Precious little hope for transformation of persons may be placed in intellectuals. The intellectual almost always broods *within* the herd, dedicating himself to mundane and sheepish idols of contentment. Despising the herd but belonging to it, he normally adds to its strength and its suppression of personhood. Only a few break free to seek the infinitely greater rewards of selfhood, and by their liberation provide the last remaining hopes for *genuine* community.

Plato, of course, understood the problem of leading individuals from captivity to understanding. Deprived of an illuminating vision of reality, the occupants of his cave must live in a world of illusion, animated by distortions that can never impel progress. No matter how vigorously they cling to their principles of "pragmatism," their truth is, as Plato says, "literally nothing but the shadows of images."

Human history begins in caves, but only when we emerge from labyrinthine passages of confusion and incoherence will we not expect an abrupt end to this history. Meandering, spiraling mazes, these caves confine us to Paleolithic corridors of mind, twisting, slippery paths on which understanding is always an intrusion. Discovering our way out of the cavern of error, the labyrinth of the world of the reigning herd, we may undergo the only serious form of reincarnation.

In the cave erected by the state the self curls up in sleep. What must come to pass before shadows give way to authentic vision? We spoke of the bargain in which the state has exchanged *things* (and consequently veiled promises of immortality) for denials of selfhood, but what must happen before this bargain is revealed for what it really is: a surrender of life's rich potentialities for submission and eventual disintegration? How can we convince millions of Americans that the demonic is polymorphous and that obsessive anti-Sovietism is a lie founded on our imprisonment by the herd?

The answer is both simple and troubling. Before Americans can draw self-esteem from their own inwardness (and thereby refuse to share in the state religion of anti-Sovietism that destroys America as a nation), they will have to discover that the bargain has not been kept. Until now, such discovery has been prevented by the "success" of our consumption-driven economy. Soon, however, increasing economic dislocation characterized by widespread unemployment and declining living standards may produce dramatic changes in the way Americans calculate the benefits of belonging.

The problems with the American economy largely reflect the world economy in general. And the world economy is in serious trouble, ridden by tensions that threaten what the World Bank in 1986 called "hesitant recovery." By early 1987 an American trade deficit that had provided almost all of the growth in world import demand for several years soared to a level that could not be sustained. To address the trade deficit, America must restore growth in world demand for our exports. This, in turn, requires a substantial improvement in the problems of third world debt, which continue to depress American markets and destroy American jobs.

The economic outlook is not sanguine. Reducing the extraordinary trade imbalances in the world economy may provoke a global recession. To move toward maximum economic growth developing nations need to import more than they export, but this must be financed by capital flows from abroad. Between 1981 and 1986 the debt crisis caused net private lending to problem countries to drop from $58 billion to a negative $1 billion. Not surprisingly, the countries deprived of finance were forced to cut imports by more than 30 percent during the period.[2]

This is merely the tip of the iceberg. We cannot assess here all the specific hazards to the economy that could produce lucidity in America. What is important is that failure to relieve the financial constraint on third world countries is increasingly likely, and that failure could lead to falling incomes in the developed world, rising protectionism, and a fall in world trade reminiscent of the 1930s.

The present shows other disturbing similarities to the decade before World War II. As economist John Kenneth Galbraith warned in the January 1987 issue of *The Atlantic*, the speculative stock market and feverish corporate buyouts of today have ominous parallels to the late 1920s and may even portend another crash. Many current prices bear no relation to the actual strength of the economy. Current patterns of "innovation" in financial structures generate debt that requires a continual stream of profits to finance, debt that may become insupportable as earnings fall. Perhaps most important, today's fevered investments often have nothing to do with improving the nation's industrial base. As Galbraith observes: "The young men who serve in the great investment houses render no service to investment decisions, product innovation, production, automation or labor relations in the companies whose securities they shuffle. . . . Mostly their operations absorb savings into an inherently sterile activity."

Ironically, many of the economic ills that may soon awaken America to its dreadful bargain between state and society are themselves a product of our misdirected foreign policy. Spurred on by the presumed need to maintain military superiority over the Soviet Union, we have sustained a level of Pentagon spending that exacerbates the twin deficits in budget and trade. Because of our dedication to realpolitik we have created a distinct government-dependent civilian sector that is inherently prone to inflation and waste—conditions resulting from rapid obsolescence, frequent product change, unstable markets, large bureaucracies beyond public control, cost-plus pricing, and retarded management efficiency.

Military expenditures have a profound cost to private capital use. A worsening drain on productive investment, these expenditures—especially as they have been fashioned by the Reagan administration—make impossible any sustained revitalization of the American industrial plant. By accepting an acceleration of a massive transfer of capital away from civilian industry to the military sector, we turn our backs on the industries we need. Unless this trend is reversed, our domestic and international competitive performance will wane even further, and the damage to our steel, automobile, textile, chemical, and other industries will become irreversible.

Instead of stimulating productivity, competitiveness, and innovation, America's commitment to arms will bring about more severe recession. The victims of such economic dislocation will include not only the most marginal elements of American society, those that the administration has begun to form into a permanent underclass, but also those comfortable segments of farmers, workers, professionals, and investors who refuse to confront the essential logic of survival in a tightening national and global marketplace.

We must understand that military spending generates a stream of buying power without producing an equivalent supply of useful goods. The excess of disposable income over available supply builds up a steady and generalized pressure on prices. Military demands also add directly to the pressure on prices for specific goods, especially when military purchases are directed to those commodities and skills in shortest supply.

Heavy military spending also absorbs resources that might have been invested more productively. While an enormous share of the budget goes to weapons, our country ignores essential research that could develop alternate sources of energy, increased food production, better housing, and improved public health. These distorted priorities perpetually limit innovation and investment, occasioning low growth, diminishing competitiveness, and the kind of trade deficit that we continue to experience.

Military spending creates a debilitating shortage of professional talent in the civilian sector. With the military sector as a whole now claiming 30 percent to 50 percent of all the scientists and engineers in America, U.S. industry is unable to contend with foreign competition. The remedy for this problem does not lie in contrived exhortations to "buy American," but in prompt disengagement from excessive spending on weapons. The American consumer who now prefers imported goods over domestic products acts not from a lack of patriotism but from an informed awareness that foreign goods are likely to be better. Before this situation can be changed, we will have to return our scientists and engineers from their Pentagon-directed laboratories and drawing-boards to operations in the capital-starved steel, automobile, and commercial electronics industries.

What will happen if individual Americans are awakened from their intellectual and moral imprisonment by economic distress and forced to confront their illusions? Consider Plato's description in book 7 of *The Republic*, where the prisoners are given their freedom to leave the cave:

> At first, when any of them is liberated and compelled suddenly to stand up and turn his neck round and walk and look towards the light, he will suffer sharp pains; the glare will distress him, and he will be unable to see the realities of which in his former state he had seen the shadows; and then conceive someone saying to him, that what he saw before was an illusion, but that now, when he is approaching nearer to being and his eye is turned towards more real existence, he has a clearer vision—what will be his reply? And you may further imagine that his instructor is pointing to the objects as they pass and requiring him to name them—will he not be perplexed? Will he not fancy that the shadows which he formerly saw are truer than the objects which are now shown to him?

"Far truer," says Plato. After a time, however, subtle changes take place. The former inhabitant of the cave grows accustomed to the sight of the upper world. Although he first saw shadows best, he now begins to see things as they really are. Challenging the errors of the den, he pities his former fellow prisoners and seeks to disabuse them of their folly.

This brings us back to an essential concern for the whole. To fulfill our vision of human transformation in America, we must aid the progressive development of individual potentials without losing sight of the cumulative effects. With Marcus Aurelius, we must never cease asking the basic questions of *Meditations:* "What is the nature of the whole, and what is my nature, and how is this related to that, and what kind of part is it of what kind of whole?"

The ascent from the herd world toward true understanding is laborious. Even after certain individuals accomplish it, this ascent is unlikely to be widely paralleled. The transference of understanding from person to polity, from part to whole, may take a long time.

Concerning the potential of the United States, we are bred into a world of thoughtlessness. But we are capable of developing our consciousness and ascending into reaches wherein personal growth is easily harmonized with the good of the whole. To unloose this capability and a purposeful foreign policy we must appreciate that a *productive* oneness (not the pseudo-unity of contemporary politics) lies hidden beneath the diversities of a seemingly fractionated world. When Hesse's Siddhartha listened attentively to his river, "he did not bind his soul to any one particular voice and absorb it in his Self, but heard them all, the Whole, the unity; then the great song of a thousand voices consisted of one word: Om—perfection."

The world is full of noise, but we can listen for real music. Like Hesse's Steppenwolf, who behind a mixture of the trumpet's bronchial slime and chewed rubber discovers the noble outline of divine music, we may "tune out" the eternal babble of politics and the herd to hear the majestic structure of the composition and full broad bowing of the strings. Caught up in a war against the individual, the murdered and murderous sounds ooze on and on, but the original spirit of music can never be destroyed. Although life in the herd seeks to strip this music of its sensuous tones, spoiling, scratching, and besliming it, for those who learn to listen even the most ghastly of disguises will give way to beauty.

Only when enough persons have learned to listen can the herds themselves be transformed. In terms of international relations, this means that the states themselves can become purposeful communities that sustain individuals, who in turn ensure harmonious and dignified foreign policies—but not until civic virtue has yielded to personhood. When this happens, states themselves will be self-affirmed and interstate conflict replaced by authentic planetization, a process whereby the presumed power of the individual state is replaced by the authentic power of the global community (not coercive military power but the power of a universalized and new consciousness, a clear vision of reality that substitutes wholeness and convergence for the fatal instincts of narcissism.) In the words of Unamuno: "Here below, in the midst of the orchestra, we hear scarcely more than the dissonances; but there above, in the heaven of art, one hears the harmonic symphony that the races, religions, languages, and countries produce, sounding separate notes, each one vibrating in its own chord with its specific timbre."[3]

All of human society can be our alma mater. With every polis a cosmopolis, humankind could be initiated into personhood and peace. Fashioning new societies based on entirely new definitions of redemption, individual Americans could emerge from Plato's cave and begin, for the first time, to look in *all* directions.

We must aim at the realization of the unique and fulfilled self in service to all others, an integral vision sparked by the impulse to survive as a nation. Rescued from our captivity in the crowd of thoughtlessness and conformity, we might then accept our liberation from a contrived struggle with the Soviet Union. Substituting productive uncertainties for the comforting lies of government, we might learn to encourage doubt as a replacement for the tranquilizing woes of belonging.

When this happens Americans will become truly free, displaying the highest forms of patriotism envisioned by the Founding Fathers. For the creators of the American republic, the true patriot was not the smug servitor of passing ideologies but rather one who was willing to measure his leaders against the immutable standards of a higher law. Challenged by the banal syntax of nuclear mandarins who speak only the language of death, tomorrow's patriot will understand that he must demand of his government a last-minute disengagement from falsehoods.

Under current conditions, faith in the herd mythology of realpolitik can serve only anguish and collapse. Reaffirming our faith in America we will be justified in only one path, the path to authentic bases of self-worth and personal meaning. Defied again and again by a leadership that must be inimical to truth, we must once again recognize ourselves as a nation of individuals.

"Nothing really changes," says Louis-Ferdinand Céline in *Journey to the End of the Night*. "Habits, ideas, opinions, we change them not at all, or if we do, we change them so late that it's no longer worth while. We are born loyal and we die of it."

We *appear* to be born loyal; in fact, we are beaten down into loyalty and self-denial only by the incessant claims of the herd. Making themselves preeminent everywhere, in every nook and cranny of social discourse and interaction, these claims crush all life between birth and death. The "highest" realm of the herd, a kingdom that demands obeisance from all other herds and that destroys individuality only because these other herds have been "successful," is politics.

All politics is delinquency, violating the rights of self-affirmation in favor of the herd. All politics are infantile, a game of Eros and Thanatos, of sex and war. It is not in the realm of politics that we must seek a change. Rather, we must change the more primary spheres that allocate feelings of self-worth. As long as these institutions defy personhood and identify success with belonging, loyalty will overshadow reason and death will overtake life.

All states usurp the power of the person, creating covenants that make assertions of individuality into a sacrilege. The remedy lies not in putting an end to states, but in creating the conditions wherein citizens can become persons. Although Nietzsche is correct that it is "for the superfluous the state was invented," humankind may still develop into a purposeful species within national boundaries. Indeed, it is through such development that the states themselves may be changed, a metamorphosis that can then "feed back" and sustain a continuing series of personal and national transformations. In terms of American foreign policy, this suggests a momentous partnership between citizen and government in which the accelerating willingness of individuals to draw meaning apart from their membership in the herd *restores* America to the world. Of course, such a partnership itself depends on a willingness of individuals to confront their own mortality, a confrontation that makes possible the rejection of inducements still held out by the state to ensure absolute conformity (inducements such as money and possessions that represent the denial of physicalness, of animality, of decay, and of death).

"Mankind," says Plotinus, "is poised midway between the gods and the beasts." More often than we care to recall, however, *Homo homini lupus* (Man is a wolf to man). Abandoning its potential for peace, our species—its dignity vitiated at the source—surrenders to perfidy. In terms of a dying U.S. foreign policy, this points uncompromisingly toward a revival of personal meaning in America, a revival that would supplant the rallying cry of anti-Sovietism with a reaffirmation of genuine ideology.

As we have seen, this revival cannot begin in the realm of politics. "Politics," Ortega y Gasset recognized, "is a second-level occupation."[4] The revival must begin as a rejection of a relentlessly degrading social and cultural life. It must begin at home, in the schools, in the work place, in the clubs, in the churches and synagogues, and in the universities.

At the moment the "crowd" is not only lonely, as David Riesman tells us,[5] but lethal. Left unchallenged as the source of private identity, it will prod us to accept any lie with indifference. Where this lie informs us that our status as Americans flows from a caricatural contest with the Soviet Union, it will push us beyond the limits of safety into the icy grip of collective annihilation.

Until now the dangers of the crowd were thought to rest only in the immediate effects of mob action. Carl Jung observed that if "people crowd together and form a mob, then the dynamics of the collective man are set free—beasts or demons which lie dormant in every person till he is part of a mob. Man in the crowd is unconsciously lowered to an inferior moral and intellectual level, to that level which is always there, below the threshold of consciousness, ready to break forth as soon as it is stimulated through the formation of a crowd."[6]

Jung's observation is certainly correct, but it misses an essential point: that is, that the crowd is *always* present; it produces its terrible effects without a physical coming-together of people; it celebrates conformity and compliance with falsehoods even as each person proceeds "independently" with his or her own affairs. The crowd is less an assembly than a condition of inconscience, a ritualized pattern of thoughtlessness defined and sustained by officials masquerading as leaders. What is more, these officials themselves believe that gibberish is truth. Captivated by the sterility of their own past, they are mostly less sinister than self-destroyed.

Nothing is to be gained from a change in leadership, from Republicans to Democrats or the other way round. Such change produces little more than a new crippled pilot for a ship that is already fixed on a collision course. If we seek a free and secure nation we must first accept the obligations of *self*-liberation. Only then will this nation take its place *within* the world, pursuing foreign policies that point not toward peril but toward planetization.

The true individual is the irreconcilable enemy not of the nation that seeks communion with all other nations, but of the herd that masquerades as a nation. Indeed, this individual is an indispensable component of every nation that seeks to endure. Without him or her the herd may call itself a nation, but the desolate crowds that comprise its population must inevitably disappear. Animated by the virtues of the solid citizen, this herd reviles thought and lionizes all who would identify patriotism with endless slaughter.

This herd is the author of suffering. Monkeys with the gift of speech, its minions learn nothing from lessons of the past, content with their fingers always round our throats, choking off the faintest hints of disapproval. At the first sounds of war they are ready to transform young men into heroes, but when the smell of death saturates the air they are the first to disappear. Louis-Ferdinand Céline relates the fate of an earlier generation trapped by such a herd in *Journey to the End of the Night*, a fate that begins when a regiment of soldiers marches past a Paris café and groups of young Frenchmen fall in behind the band:

> We went on marching for a long time. There were streets then there were still more streets, with civilians and their wives cheering us as we passed, and throwing flowers to us from the café tables, by the stations and from the steps of crowded churches. What a lot of patriots there were! And then, after a bit, there began to be fewer patriots. . . . Rain came down, and there were fewer and fewer of them, and then finally no one cheered at all, not another cheer along the road. Were we all by ourselves then? A column of men, in fours, behind each other? The music stopped. Then I said to myself, as I saw how things were going, "Its not such fun, after all. I doubt if its worth it." And I was going to go back. But it was too late! They'd shut the gate behind us, quietly; the civilians had. We were caught, like rats in a trap.

After his first visit to the United States in 1842, Charles Dickens wrote: "I do fear that the heaviest blow ever dealt at liberty will be dealt by this country in the failure of its example to the earth."[7] For the moment, Dickens's fear seems to have been well founded. Tossing about without any sense of real understanding, our country continues to languish *outside* the world, content that its passions are inauthentic and that its citizens draw meaning from the absence of thought. Yet for all of its blemishes America still nurtures hope. At the end of *The Future in America*, H. G. Wells wrote: "It seems to me that in America, by sheer virtue of its size, its free traditions, and the habit of initiative in its people, the leadership of progress must ultimately rest."[8] If Wells is to be proven correct, America will first have to become more lucid and less "prosperous."

A passage in the *Odyssey* speaks of two gates, one of horn and one of ivory. Through the ivory gate false dreams pass to humankind, and through the gate of horn go the true and prophetic dreams. Until now, America has stood forlornly before the ivory gate, content with imaginings of greatness that direct us toward disappearance. To move before the gate of horn is still possible, but only if the I, as subject, reappears. Before America can be restored to the world, Americans must be restored to themselves. There is no other way.

Notes

1. The Faust legend probably has its origins in the story of a practicing magician who allegedly worked sensational wonders and died scandalously in 1537. This sorcerer is the hero of the German *Faust-Book*, published fifty years after his death. Goethe did not see this book, but Christopher Marlowe did and adapted it for his *Tragedy of Doctor Faustus*, a study of the scholar in search of unlimited knowledge and the power that knowledge may confer. In modern literature the Faust legend reached its highest form in Goethe's *Faust*. Investing the legend with intellectual and spiritual values going far beyond the old crudities of devilry and punishment, Goethe created a dramatic poem exploring the troubled human soul common to us all, examining courage in the face of an unbearable fate and inquiring whether true fulfillment can ever coexist with egoism. The main theme of the work, Faust as contractor with the devil for superhuman earthly powers, has put the adjective *Faustian* into general English use, describing a bargain in which the loss of one's soul is exchanged for short-term secular advantages (although Goethe's Faust emerges from the depths of his experience as a passionate human spirit, preserving his soul when it is borne away by the heavenly host). A history of the individual judged by the metaphysics of human aspiration, Faust has figured in numerous post-Goethean works including Gounod's opera and Thomas Mann's *Doktor Faustus*.

2. See David R. Obey and Paul S. Sarbanes, "'Recycling' Surpluses to the Third World," *New York Times*, November 9, 1986, F3.
3. See Miguel de Unamuno, *Contra Esto Y Aquello* (Buenos Aires: Espasa-Calpe, 1941), 133; cited by Michael A. Weinstein, "Singularity and Transcendence in Unamuno's Political Thought," unpublished mimeo, Purdue University (1986), 17.
4. See José Ortega y Gasset, *Invertebrate Spain* (Madrid, 1922).
5. See David Riesman, *The Lonely Crowd* (New Haven: Yale University Press, 1961).
6. See C. G. Jung, "Psychology and Religion," in G. B. Levitas, *The World of Psychology*, vol. 2, *Identity and Motivation* (New York: George Braziller, 1963), 476–77.
7. See Marc Pachter, ed., *Abroad in America: Visitors to the New Nation 1776–1914*, (Reading, Mass.: Addison-Wesley in association with the National Portrait Gallery, Smithsonian Institution, 1976).
8. Ibid., 301.

Index

About the Author

Louis René Beres, professor of political science at Purdue University, received his Ph.D. at Princeton in 1971. A noted specialist in foreign affairs and international law with particular reference to strategic studies, he is the author of many major books and articles in the field. Beres is a frequent lecturer in the United States and abroad on nuclear weapons and nuclear war. He is recognized internationally as one of the world's leading scholars in the movement for a durable and just peace. Professor Beres's forthcoming book is *Earth's Body: Self-Affirmation and World Order.*